WORLD SOILS

D0552673

E. M. BRIDGES

Senior Lecturer in Geography
at the University College of Swansea

WORLD SOILS

SECOND EDITION

CAMBRIDGE
UNIVERSITY PRESS

Published by the Press Syndicate of the University of Cambridge
The Pitt Building, Trumpington Street, Cambridge CB2 1RP
40 West 20th Street, New York, NY 10011–4211, USA
10 Stamford Road, Oakleigh, Victoria 3166, Australia

© Cambridge University Press 1970, 1978

First published 1970
Fourth printing 1976
Second edition 1978
Seventh printing 1993

Printed in Malta by Interprint Limited

Library of Congress Cataloguing in Publication Data

Bridges, Edwin Michael.
World soils.
Bibliography: P.
Includes index.
1. Soil science.   1. Title.
S591.B85   1978   631.4   77-90204

ISBN 0 521 29339 1 paperback

(First edition ISBN 0 521 07616 1)

CONTENTS

The colour plates are between pages 64 and 65

PREFACE TO THE SECOND EDITION

The second edition of this book, like the first, attempts to provide students of agriculture, biology, geography, environmental science and soil science with an introduction to the study of the soils of the world. It is specifically directed at students who are in their last years at school or are taking courses in colleges or universities at an introductory level. The policy of the author has been to convey information concisely and with the minimum of pedological jargon. The book aims to give the student a satisfactory basis of knowledge upon which further studies can be built if so desired. Although information has been obtained from many sources throughout the world, the presentation reflects the British approach and background of the author.

In preparing this edition for the press, the opportunity has been taken to incorporate a number of modifications into the text. The factors and processes of soil formation have been placed in separate chapters to stress the importance of the internal processes which are responsible for soil profile development. The chapter on soil classification has been brought up to date and now includes reference to both U.S. Soil Taxonomy and the Legend of the F.A.O./U.N.E.S.C.O. Soil Map of the World as well as the current British system of soil classification. Synonyms of soils have been introduced where practicable to familiarise readers with these international systems of soil classification. The chapter concerned with soil mapping now serves as a link between the soils described and their distribution, fertility, land use capability and other applications of soil science which are discussed in the last chapter. Whilst not departing radically from the first edition it is hoped that these changes will improve the usefulness of the book and bring it up to date.

E. M. Bridges
University College of Swansea,
Natural Science Building,
Singleton Park,
SWANSEA SA2 8PP

ACKNOWLEDGEMENTS

The author wishes to acknowledge the help given by the following: Mrs G. Bridges for drawing the diagrams, G. B. Lewis for compiling the world soil map, C. P. Burnham, H. Vine, and A. Young for their helpful comments and suggestions, Mrs S. E. Shackleton Bailey for secretarial assistance, D. E. Price and A. F. Cutliffe for photographic assistance and the Geography Department of the University College of Swansea for the use of its facilities.

Thanks are due to D. E. Cotton for permission to reproduce Plate 1, to B. Clayden for Plate 11, to A. Young for Plate 19 and to D. Gunary for Plate 25. The other colour plates are by the author.

For permission to reproduce diagrams and photographs, thanks are due to the following: S. R. Eyre for Figs. 1.1 and 2.7 from *Vegetation and Soils*, Edward Arnold, 1969; H. O. Buckman and N. C. Brady for Figs. 2.1, 2.4b and 2.9 from *The Nature and Properties of Soils*, Macmillan, 1960; U.S.D.A. for Figs. 2.2 and 2.8 from Soil Survey Staff, *Soil Survey Manual*, 1951 and for Fig. 3.9 (a photo by W. M. Johnson) from *Soil Classification, A Comprehensive System 7th Approximation*, 1960; G. P. C. Chambers for Fig. 2.4a from 'Natural Colloidal Silicates' in *Science News* 40, Penguin Books, 1956; P. Duchafour for Fig. 2.5 from *Précis de Pédologie*, Masson et Cie, 1965; E. J. Russell for Fig. 3.3 from *The World of the Soil*, Collins Fontana Library, 1961; G. R. Clarke for Fig. 5.3 from *The Study of Soil in the Field*, Clarendon Press, 1961; Van Riper for Fig. 6.1 From *Man's Physical World*, McGraw Hill; Australian C.S.I.R.O. for Fig. 5.4 from R. A. Perry *et al.*, *General Report on Lands of the Alice Springs Area 1956–7*, 1962 and for Fig. 9.1 from *Periodic Phenomena in Landscapes as a Basis for Soil Studies*, 1959; A. K. Lobeck for Fig. 8.6 from *Geomorphology*, McGraw Hill; B. T. Bunting for Fig. 10.8 from *The Geography of the Soil*, Hutchinson University Library, 1965. Fig. 5.1 is partly based upon a map which appeared in *Efficient Use of Fertilizers*, F.A.O., 1958 and includes modifications derived from Ganssen and Hädrich *Atlas zur Bodenkunde*, Bibliographisches Institute Mannheim, Kartographisches Institute Meyer, 1965.

The author acknowledges with gratitude the factual information derived from the following sources: Brady, N. C., 1974, *The Nature and Properties of Soils*, Macmillan; Buol, S. W., McCracken, R. J. and Hole, F. D., 1973, *Soil Genesis and Classification*, Iowa State University Press, Ames; Soil Survey Staff (England and Wales) *Field Handbook*, Harpenden; Soil Survey Staff (U.S.A.), 1975, *Soil Taxonomy Handbook* No. 436 U.S.D.A., Washington; Gerasimov, I. P. and Glazovskaya, M. A., 1965, *Fundamentals of Soil Science and Soil Geography*. Trans. A Gourevich, I.P.S.T., Jerusalem.

Soil profile descriptions quoted as examples in the text are taken from the following sources: Afanasyeva, E. A., *et al.*, 1964, *Short Guide to Soil Excursion Moscow-Kherson* VIII Int. Cong. Soil Sci., Ministry of Agriculture, Moscow (descriptions by E. A. Afanasyeva, V. M. Fridland, G. S. Grin and V. D. Kissel); Tours Guide, Australian Soil Science Conference, 1966, Brisbane; Aubert, G. and Boulaine, J., 1967, *La Pédologie. Que Sais-je?* Presses Universitaires de France, Paris (descriptions by G. Aubert and N. Federoff); Bleakley, D. and Khan, E. J. A., 1963, 'Observations on the white sand areas of the Berbice Formation', British Guiana, *J. Soil Sci.*, 14, 44–51; Bridges, E. M., 1966, *The Soils and Land Use of the District north of Derby*, Mem. Soil Survey of Great Britain, Harpenden; D'Hoore, J. L., 1964, *Soil Map of Africa*, 1:5,000,000, C.T.C.A., Lagos (descriptions by J. V. Botelho da Costa, J. H. Durand, R. Frankart, J. Hervieu, N. Leneuf and G. Riou, R. Maignien and C. R. Van der Merwe); Mackney, D. and Burnham, C. P., 1964, *The Soils of the West Midlands*, Bull. no. 2, Soil Survey of Great Britain, Harpenden; Mückenhausen, E., 1956, 'Typologische Bodenentwicklung und Bodenfruchtbarkeit', pp. 37–103, in *Arbeitsgemeinschaft fur Forschung des Lands Nordrhein-Westfalen*, Westdeutscher Verlag, Köln; Mulcahy, M., 1960, 'Laterites and Lateritic soils in Southwestern Australia', *J. Soil Sci.*, 11, pp. 206–25; Northcote, K. H., *et al.*, 1954, *Soils and Land Use in the Barossa District, South Australia*, Soils and Land Use Series No. 13, C.S.I.R.O., Melbourne; Oakes, H., 1954, *The Soils of Turkey*, Ministry of Agriculture, Ankara; Soil Survey Staff, 1951, 'Soil Survey Manual', *Agricultural Handbook* No. 18, U.S.D.A., Washington; Svatkov, N. M., 1958, 'Soils of Wrangel Island', *Soviet Soil Science*, pp. 80–7; Tedrow, J. C. F. and Hill, D. E., 1955, 'Arctic Brown Soil', *Soil Science* 80, pp. 265–75; Thorp, J., 1957, *Report on a Field Study of Soils of Australia*, Earlham College, Richmond, Indiana (Mimeo); Zalibekov, Z. G., 1965,

'Separation of cinnamon-brown soils on the Aktashsk Sub-montane Dagestan Plain', *Soviet Soil Science*, pp. 1158–65; Findlay, D. C., 1965, *Soils of the Mendip District of Somerset*, Mem. Soil Survey of England and Wales, Harpenden; Targulian, V. O., *et al.*, 1974, *Arrangement, composition and genesis of sod-pale podzolic soil derived from mantle loams*, I.S.S.S., Moscow; Adu, S. V. and Tenadu, D. O., 1975, *Field tour within the forest–savanna transition and the interior savanna zones*, I.S.S.S., Ghana; F.A.O./U.N.E.S.C.O. *Soil Map of the World*, 1971 Vol. IV South America, 1975 Vol. III Mexico and Central America.

1 INTRODUCTION

Soil has a peculiar fascination, which impinges upon all of us at some time or other. Farmers or horticulturalists till it, engineers move it about in Juggernaut-like machines, small boys dig in it, and mothers abhor it as being dirty. Unfortunately, for many people soil is synonymous with dirt. They should know better, for the soil has a vital and important role to play in the life of the world and mankind. As Sir John Russell has written, 'a clod of earth seems at first sight to be the embodiment of the stillness of death'; however, he goes on to show that it is in fact a highly organised physical, chemical and biological complex on which all of us are dependent. As the support of vegetable life, the soil plays the most fundamental of roles in providing sustenance for all animals and man.

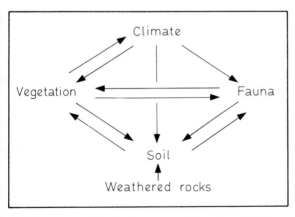

1.1 The arrows indicate the various interactions of the environment which affect the soil

The position of soil in the biotic complex can be illustrated in diagram (Fig. 1.1) where it can be seen that climate influences plants, animals and soil directly. Plants influence the soil, animals and the climate near the ground. Animals play a con-

siderable role in soil development and often the type of soil influences the animals which are present in it; animals also influence the vegetation which is growing in the soil. Finally climate, through weathering, influences the rocks, which in time become part of the soil as it is first weathered and later acted upon by soil-forming processes.

The study of soils is the occupation of the *pedologist*, and his science of *pedology* emphasises the study of the soil as a natural phenomenon on the surface of the earth. The pedologist is interested in the appearance of the soil, its mode of formation, its physical, chemical and biological composition, and its classification and distribution.

Pedology makes use of a large number of branches of scientific knowledge, and as an integrative science resembles the role of geography. As will already be apparent from the previous paragraph, aspects of physics, chemistry and biology have an important contribution to make to the study of the soil, so have studies in agriculture, forestry, history, geography, mineralogy, archaeology and geology. From all of these are obtained information which can be synthesised to make a scientific discipline and natural philosophy separate from, and yet closely related to, many other branches of natural science.

Pedology can be studied as a pure science in which the identification of the processes producing the soil profile as well as the mapping and classification of soils form an important part. However, the results obtained in the pure science can be applied to practical problems in agriculture, horticulture, forestry, engineering, and in planning the future use of the land.

In cases of the proposed development of virgin lands or of lands previously used for extensive grazing, the pedologist can offer recommendations for the cultivation practices and the parcelling out of farm units within the developing area.

9

This type of work is particularly useful in irrigation schemes where the high cost of installation makes a knowledge of the soils essential before the civil engineering work is even planned. The classification of soils leads naturally to land capability, hence the pedologist's interest in the natural fertility of soils, and the ways in which this fertility can be put to the best use or even increased.

Definition of soil

Present-day soil science has emerged from two different schools of thought, one chemical, the other geological. The German scientist Liebig was probably the most renowned exponent of the chemical view of the soil, but even before Liebig, a Swedish scientist Berzelius described soil as 'the chemical laboratory of nature in whose bosom various chemical decomposition and synthesis reactions take place in a hidden manner'. Early pedologists with a geological background considered the soil to be comminuted rock with a certain amount of organic matter derived from the decomposition products of plants. As late as 1917, a German scientist, Ramann, described soil as 'rocks that have been reduced to small fragments and have been more or less changed chemically, together with the remains of plants or animals that live in it or on it'.

Current definitions of soil result mainly from the work of two men, in Russia, Dokuchaiev, and in America, Hilgard. Independently both noted that soils were related in a general way to climate, and that soils could be described in broad geographical zones, which at the scale of world maps could be correlated not only with climate but also with the associated belts of vegetation. Although this is only partly true, it did serve to direct attention to the environmental relationships of the soil cover of our planet. This environmental approach still holds true today but it has become clear that climate, although important, is only one of a number of factors in soil formation (p. 24). The variation of soils brought to light at larger scales of mapping in many different regions of the world shows that the soil pattern results from the interplay of climate with the other soil forming factors. In this sense, soils can be considered as being in a state of dynamic equilibrium or slow evolution.

The soil can be envisaged also as an open system through which the various hydrological, biological and geochemical cycles operate. The soil forms a specific type of open system known as a process–response system in which there is a close relationship between morphological structure and the inputs and outputs of mass and energy (Fig. 3.6). These inputs and outputs usually operate in a vertical direction at any one

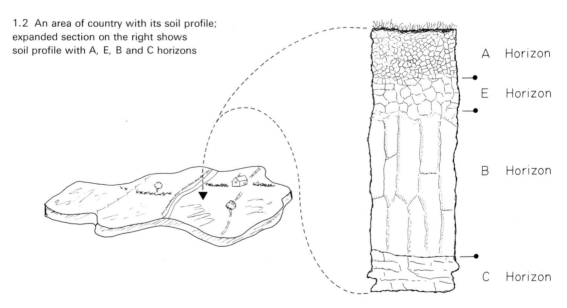

1.2 An area of country with its soil profile; expanded section on the right shows soil profile with A, E, B and C horizons

A Horizon

E Horizon

B Horizon

C Horizon

place on level surfaces but where slopes occur a horizontal component is introduced which finds expression in the different morphological properties of soil on slopes (pp. 26, 101).

The definition of soil propounded by Joffe has the advantage that it combines the physical, chemical and biological constituents, and throws the right amount of weight on the importance of morphology in the description of a soil.

'The soil is a natural body of animal, mineral and organic constituents differentiated into horizons of variable depth which differ from the material below in morphology, physical make-up, chemical properties and composition, and biological characteristics'. A more simple definition states that soil is 'the stuff in which plants grow'; however, this is not necessarily a full definition as everyone knows cress will grow on a damp piece of flannel without the aid of soil, and by the science of hydroponics many plants can be grown in water to which has been added the necessary mineral nutrients.

The succession of *horizons* which is exposed when a vertical cut is made through the soil to the parent material comprises the *soil profile* (Fig. 1.2). Since Dokuchaiev first labelled soil horizons A, B, C, a conventional notation has evolved which facilitates ease of discussion, comparison and classification. Horizons are designated according to their position in the soil profile and the processes which have brought them into being. The following notation has been adopted for *major soil horizons* in Britain and it accords with international usage.

Where present, superficial organic horizons are designated by the letters L, F, H and O; surface eluvial horizons by A and E; subsurface illuvial horizons by B; the parent material C, and unweathered rock is indicated by the letter R.

L. Fresh litter, original plant structure evident.
F. Partly decomposed and comminuted litter of previous years' growth.
H. Well decomposed material, plant structures no longer evident.
O. Peaty: plant remains accumulated under wet conditions.
A. Mineral soil horizon formed at or near the surface, characterised by incorporation of humified organic matter intimately associated with the mineral fraction. Incorporation of organic matter is presumed to result from biological activity or artificial mixing during tillage.
E. Subsurface mineral horizon underlying the A horizon that is lighter in colour and contains less organic matter, sesquioxides of iron and/or clay than the horizon beneath.
B. The B horizon is normally differentiated from adjacent horizons by colour and structure. It usually underlies an A or E horizon and is characterised by illuvial concentration of silicate clay, iron, aluminium or humus. Other forms of B horizon result from alteration of the parent material by removal of carbonates, formation, liberation or residual accumulation of silicate clays or oxides.
C. Unconsolidated or weakly consolidated mineral horizon which retains evidence of rock structure and lacks the properties diagnostic of the overlying A, E, and B horizons. The C horizon may possess accumulations of carbonates or more soluble salts; it may have dense, brittle properties and it may be modified by gleying.
R. Continuous hard or very hard bedrock.

The major soil horizons have many specific characteristics which are designated by the addition of lower case letters. These specific features are briefly described below and the processes which cause their formation are discussed in Chapter 4.

O horizons are peaty horizons accumulated under wet conditions.
They may be subdivided into:

Of	fibrous peat
Om	semi fibrous peat
On	amorphous peat

A horizons may be subdivided into:

Ah	uncultivated A horizon
Ap	cultivated A horizon
Ag	gleyed A horizon

E horizons may be subdivided into:

Ea	bleached horizon of podzol soils
Eb	lighter coloured horizon, depleted of clay and sesquioxides in brown soils
Eg	gleyed E horizon

B horizons may be subdivided into:

Bfe	thin iron pan
Bs	ochreous-coloured, sesquioxide enriched B horizon of temperate soils
Bw or (B)	'weathered' B horizon without illuvial additions
Bt	clay-enriched B horizon
Bx	compact dense fragipan
Bh	organic matter enriched B horizon
Bg	gleyed B horizon
Bca	enriched with calcium carbonate
Bir or Box	enrichment with sesquioxides in tropical soils

C horizons may be subdivided into:

Ca	unconsolidated materials
Cca	enriched with calcium carbonate
Ccs	enriched with gypsum
Cg	gleyed C horizon
CG	strongly gleyed horizon which changes colour on exposure to air
Cx	compact, dense fragipan
Cm	cemented material

The symbols used to represent soil horizons throughout this book are given in Fig. 1.3. The presence of certain horizons and their order in the soil profile indicatees which soil forming process

	L	Undecomposed litter
	F	Partially-decomposed litter
	H	Well-decomposed humus layer, low in mineral matter
	A	Acid incorporated humus
	A	Neutral or calcareous, incorporated humus
	Ea	Bleached horizon of podzolized soils
	Eag	Bleached, gleyed horizon of podzolized soils
	Ebg	Bleached, gleyed horizon of gley soils
	Eb	Eluvial horizon depleted of clay and/or sesquioxides
	Bh	Horizon of maximum humus deposition in podzolized soils
	Bfe	Horizon of maximum iron deposition in podzolized soils
	(B) or Bw	Weathered horizon without appreciable enrichment in colloidal material
	B	Undifferentiated illuvial horizon
	Bt	Horizon containing illuviated clay (textural B horizon)
	Bir	Sesquioxide-enriched horizon of tropical soils
	Bs	Sesquioxide-enriched horizon of temperate soils
	Bg	Illuvial horizon with strong gleying features
	Bt/Bir	Sesquioxide- and clay-enriched horizon of tropical soils
	C	Calcareous parent material
	C	Non-calcareous parent material
	Cg	Parent material with strong features of gleying
	Bca or Cca	Horizons enriched with calcium carbonate

1.3 Symbols used to represent soil horizons thoughout this book. These symbols are not used by all soil scientists in their interpretation of soil profiles. Consequently, not all examples used in this book have them. Combinations of symbols indicate a horizon with features common to both are operating. A discussion of the factors which control these processes occurs in Chapter 3.

Soils are developed in material which has already been weathered from the solid rocks. This *weathered mantle* or *regolith* can be as deep as 50 m. in the humid tropics. In Britain and northern Europe the depth is variable, but on average is somewhere around 1 to 1.5 m. although in places it is non-existent. Before attempting an account of the soils of the world it is necessary to know something of the ways in which soils are classified. These are dealt with in Chapter 5. The soils of the world are described in broad latitudinal zones in Chapters 6 to 9 and the intra- zonal and azonal soils in Chapter 10. Examples of soil profiles from published and unpublished sources are given as illustrations of different soil types. The original author's description has been retained where possible, but some rearrangement and simplification has often been necessary. This accounts for the variability of the different descriptions.

The different approaches to mapping soils are discussed in Chapter 11 together with the methods of soil description and sampling in common use. A discussion of world soil distributions, soil fertility, land use capability and other applied uses of soil data concludes the book.

2 COMPOSITION OF SOILS

There are four main constituents of soil: mineral matter, organic matter, air and water (Fig. 2.1). The mineral matter includes all those minerals weathered from the parent material as well as those formed in the soil by recombination from substances in the soil solution. The organic matter is derived mostly from decaying vegetable matter which is broken down and decomposed by the action of the many different forms of animal life which live in the soil. Normally both air and water occupy the spaces between the structures of the soil, but if a soil is saturated with water most of the air is driven out. In a soil which is freely drained some water is still present in the form of thin films around the mineral particles, leaving the spaces of the fissures and pores open for the penetration of the atmosphere.

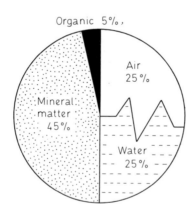

2.1 Volume composition of a typical topsoil; amounts are approximate as the percentage of certain constituents, e.g. air and water, is constantly varying

Mineral matter
The mineral portion of soil is derived from the parent material by weathering and consists of a range of particle sizes from very small clay par-

ticles of less than 0.002 mm. diameter to sand-size particles of up to 2 mm. diameter. This part of the soil is known as the *fine earth* and it is upon this that the *texture* of the soil is determined. Larger particles or stones occur also, but except for their bulk are considered to be inert, contributing only by their physical presence. This can be useful in a fine-textured soil in that the stones break the continuity of the clay material. Taking the three different fractions of sand, silt and clay which occur in any soil, it is possible to relate them to the triangular diagram (Fig. 2.2a). The texture of a soil can easily be determined in the field by first moistening and then estimating the proportions of sand, silt and clay as it is worked between finger and thumb. (Sand 2 mm.–0.05 mm., silt 0.05–0.002 mm., clay < 0.002 mm.) Descriptions of the different classes of soil texture are given in Table 2.1.

Table 2.1   Soil texture class descriptions

Sand. Soil consisting mostly of coarse and fine sand, and containing so little clay that it is loose when dry and not sticky at all when wet. When rubbed it leaves no film on the fingers.

Loamy sand. Consisting mostly of sand but with sufficient clay to give slight plasticity and cohesion when very moist. Leaves a slight film of fine materials on the fingers when rubbed.

Sandy loam. Soil in which the sand fraction is still quite obvious, which moulds readily when sufficiently moist but in most cases does not stick appreciably to the fingers. Threads do not form easily.

Loam. Soil in which the fractions are so blended that it moulds readily when sufficiently moist, and sticks to the fingers to some extent. It can with difficulty be moulded into threads but will not bend into a small ring.

Silt loam. Soil that is moderately plastic without being very sticky and in which the smooth soapy feel of the silt is the main feature.

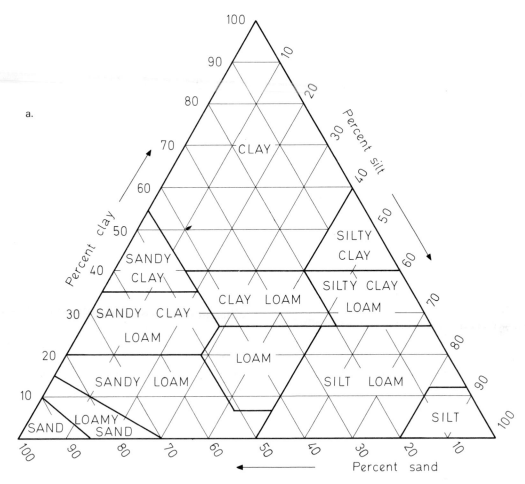

2.2 (a) Soil texture classes, U.S.D.A. The three sides represent base lines for sand, silt and clay with the apices opposite representing 100 per cent of each constituent. Percentages can be read off to give the textural name for any soil sample. (b) Broad soil texture groupings. (c) Soil texture classes, Soil Survey of England and Wales.

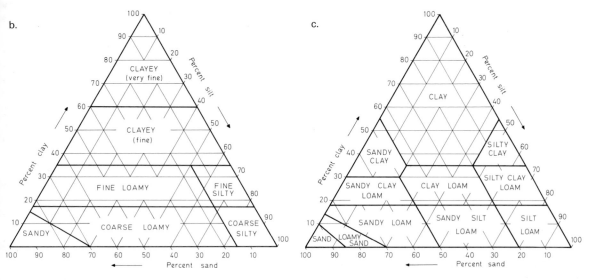

Sandy clay loam. Soils containing sufficient clay to be distinctly sticky when moist, but in which the sand fraction is still an obvious feature.

Clay loam. The soil is distinctly sticky when sufficiently moist, and the presence of sand fractions can only be detected with care.

Silty clay loam. This contains quite subordinate amounts of sand, but sufficient silt to confer something of a smooth soapy feel. It is less sticky than silty clay or clay loam.

Silt. Soil in which the smooth, soapy feel of silt is dominant.

Sandy clay. The soil is plastic and sticky when moistened sufficiently, but the sand fraction is still an obvious feature. Clay and sand are dominant, and the intermediate grades of silt and very fine sand are less apparent.

Clay. The soil is plastic and sticky when moistened sufficiently and gives a polished surface on rubbing. When moist the soil can be rolled into threads, and it is capable of being moulded into any shape and takes clear fingerprints.

Silty clay. Soil which is composed almost entirely of very fine material but in which the smooth soapy feel of the silt fraction modifies to some extent the stickiness of the clay.

These texture classes are used for the description of texture within a profile but there is a need for broader groupings of soil textures when describing the whole profile or groups of similar soils. These textural groupings are:

clayey	very fine
	fine
silty	fine
	coarse
loamy	fine
	coarse
sandy	

The relationship of the twelve texture classes to these seven textural groupings can be seen in the second triangular diagram (Fig. 2.2b). These broad textural groupings cut across several of the textural classes as they are based upon slightly different particle sizes. This has occurred because of the need for closer co-operation between engineers and soil scientists which has resulted in the pedological size grades being modified according to a scale having sand 2.00 mm. to 0.06 mm.; silt 0.06 mm. to < 0.002 mm. and clay 0.002 mm.

2.3 Some of the less common (heavy) minerals present in the soil: (a), (b), zircon; (d), (e), (f), garnet; (g), tourmaline; (h), iron ore (magnetite)

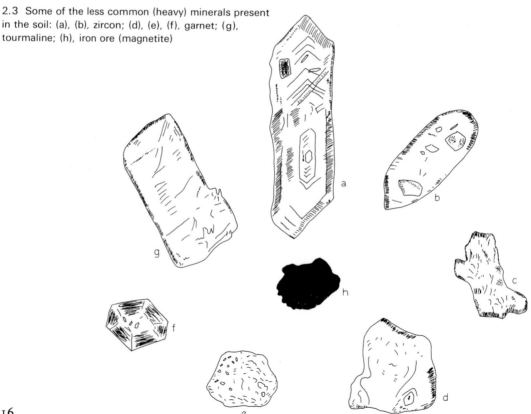

This obviously necessitated some changes in the texture classes to conform with the new size grades. The scheme adopted by the Soil Survey of England and Wales is given in the third triangular diagram (Fig. 2.2c). Where stony material amounts to more than 35 per cent of the volume of a soil horizon, it is necessary to indicate this in the textural description. The term *skeletal* (in England and Wales) or *fragmental* (U.S.A.) can be used in conjunction with the appropriate textural grouping.

These different soil textures have properties which affect the management and economic use of the soil. Coarse-textured, sandy soils are usually freely drained, and in a dry summer may suffer from drought, but cultivation is relatively easy. Frequently, clay soils are poorly drained, and the expense of installing a drainage system can be large. Cultivations are always likely to be difficult, although in a dry year these soils may produce better crops than a sandy soil. Silty soils are also troublesome in that they must be cultivated within certain moisture limits, otherwise they come cloddy and the preparation of a seed bed is made difficult. Also, the effect of heavy rain causes surface-sealing which inhibits seedling emergence, and encourages sheet erosion.

The minerals present in a soil usually have been through at least one cycle of weathering so that only the most resistant ones remain. In a humid temperate environment, the sand fraction is composed largely of quartz particles, but it also contains felspars, micas and a number of rarer minerals such as zircon, tourmaline, or glauconite (Fig. 2. 3). These minerals can sometimes be used to determine the origin of the parent material, and other minerals such as the oxides of iron including magnetite, haematite and limonite commonly occur. Quartz grains often comprise between 90 and 95 per cent of all the silt and sand particles in soils derived from sedimentary rocks.

In most soils developed in a humid tropical environment, weatherable minerals such as felspar and mica are virtually absent. Kaolinite, together with iron oxides and sometimes aluminium hydroxide make up the clay fraction, with a variable proportion of quartz sand but there is little silt.

The clay minerals are the most important mineral constituents of soils; they consist of very

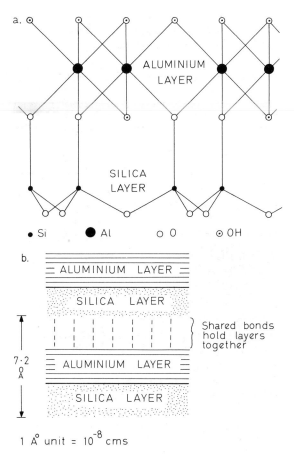

• Si   ● Al   ○ O   ⊙ OH

$1 \text{ Å unit} = 10^{-8} \text{ cms}$

2.4 (a) Arrangement of the atoms in the clay mineral kaolinite; (b) Diagrammatic representation of the layered structure typical of the clay minerals

small platy-structured mineral fragments which can be identified only indirectly or by an electron microscope. Clay minerals are members of a group of minerals which are characterised by a layered, crystalline structure. There are three main members of this group of minerals, *kaolinite*, *montmorillonite* and the *hydrous micas*, although other transitional forms occur between each type. All the clay minerals are built up from layers of silica and aluminium atoms with their attendant oxygen atoms arranged like a sandwich (Fig. 2.4). The layers of the sandwich are held together by chemical bonds shared between the different layers.

Some minerals are formed in the soil itself. Weathering releases elements from the minerals and they pass into the soil solution from which recrystallisation takes place forming new minerals. Hence kaolinite can be formed in this way from soil solutions rich in aluminium and silicon. Where base-rich conditions prevail the mineral montmorillonite may be formed. Clay minerals can also be formed in the soil by alteration of the primary minerals. Other secondary minerals can accumulate in the soil. Where gleying is prevalent concretions of iron and manganese oxides occur scattered throughout the subsoil horizons of some surface-water gley soils. These grow by the addition of concentric layers of iron and manganese compounds. Concretions of calcareous material are unusual in Britain and other humid countries because of the leaching which takes place, but they are common in the soils of drier climates such as in the chernozems of the steppes of Russia.

Because the clay mineral particles are so small in size, the minute electrical forces of the molecules at the surface of the clay become dominant and confer upon the clay particles a *colloidal* condition. A colloidal state occurs when particles of less than one micron (0.001 mm.) in size are dispersed evenly throughout another material. (Two common examples of colloids are milk, in which tiny solid particles are dispersed throughout a liquid, and cloud, where water droplets are dispersed throughout a gaseous mixture.) Properties which are conferred upon a soil by the colloidal state are plasticity, cohesion, shrinkage, swelling, flocculation and dispersion (Fig. 2.5).

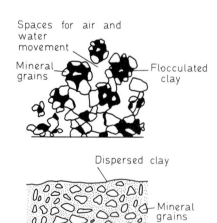

Spaces for air and water movement

Mineral grains

Flocculated clay

Dispersed clay

Mineral grains

2.5 The effect of flocculation and dispersion on soil. The flocculated soil is well structured and has spaces through which air and water can move. These spaces are lost or very much reduced when a soil is dispersed

Organic matter

Soil organic matter can take several forms: it may be intimately mixed with the mineral matter of the surface horizon, it may be present in an illuvial Bh horizon, or it may lie upon the surface. The four main types of surface organic matter are known as *peat*, *mull*, *moder* and *mor* (Fig. 2.6).

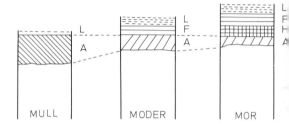

2.6 Diagrammatic representation of the thin surface forms of organic matter accumulation in soils

Gradational forms can be recognised between these types though they remain closely related to the basic varieties.

Accumulations of organic matter under wet, anaerobic conditions are known as peat. The name peat is used for accumulations which are more than 40 cm. thick with fibrous, semifibrous and amorphous forms being recognised. With thinner forms such as occur in many upland areas in the west of the British Isles the adjective humic is used in conjunction with the name of the underlying mineral soil.

Mor develops best beneath a heathland or coniferous forest plant community. As the litter, L, which falls from the plants is low in base content, strong acidity rapidly develops which inhibits the activity of the soil fauna. Breakdown is retarded so that the litter accumulates to form a transition or fermentation F horizon with increasingly matted material towards the base of the horizon. A thin horizon of completely humidified and amorphous material forms the humus, H, horizon. As the activity of the soil fauna is restricted in this type of organic matter, much of the breakdown is achieved by the action of fungi. Earthworms are usually absent so that incorporation of the humus into the mineral soil is extremely slow.

Moder is a form of organic matter intermediate between mor and mull, having a richer soil fauna than mor. It comprises decomposing organic matter and faecal pellets of the soil fauna, especially those of springtails and mites. Litter and fermentation horizons are identifiable in approximately equal thicknesses, and in the case of forms transitional to mull, some incorporation into the mineral soil occurs as well.

Mull forms in freely drained, base-rich soils with good aeration. As these conditions are good for plant life as well, there is a plentiful supply of plant litter, and associated with it a rich soil fauna including earthworms. The organic debris is completely broken down and humified each year so that none remains from one year to the next. Earthworms, in particular, are responsible for ingesting the plant material and intimately mixing it with the mineral part of the soil. When in the mull form, the humus is finely divided (colloidal) and is intimately associated with the mineral soil, especially the clay with which it forms the *clay-humus* complex.

The clay-humus complex

The chemistry of the soil is concerned largely with the chemical and physical activity of these minute particles of the clay-humus complex. As long ago as 1850 Thomas Way found that soils had the power to retain cations and that natural clays reacted in a similar manner to artificial silicates of lime and aluminium. Subsequent work has shown this piece of research to have been correct, but the mechanism was not understood at the time. Acids, alkalies and their salts when in solution dissociate to a certain degree, that is they form *ions* with positive and negative charges. Water has the same property, dissociating into a hydrogen ion H^+ and a hydroxide ion OH^-.

$$NaNO_3 \rightleftharpoons Na^+ + NO_3^-$$
$$H_2O \rightleftharpoons H^+ + OH^-$$

Because of the broken edges of the silicate clay crystals and ionic substitution within their structure, the clay mineral particles have a net negative charge. The clay-humus particle effectively acts as a highly charged anion, which, in colloidal chemistry is known as a *micelle*. Surrounding the micelle and attracted to it by the negative charge are numerous adsorbed cations (Fig. 2.7). These

adsorbed cations surrounding the micelle are capable of being exchanged for others. The total amount of exchangeable ions is known as the total exchange capacity of the soil.

The process of leaching is in effect the continual adsorption of hydrogen or aluminium ions in place of the calcium and other bases. These are displaced by the mass action of hydrogen ions present in carbonated water and the acid breakdown products of plant litter and of aluminium ions dissolved from the clay minerals themselves in the acid conditions. The soils of the humid temperate regions tend to be saturated with the ions of hydrogen and calcium as well as with lesser numbers of magnesium and potassium ions. In the humid tropics aluminium ions play an important part. With increasing dryness of climate and less leaching, calcium and magnesium ions dominate the exchange positions of the clays as in the chernozem soils. Where leaching is minimal and the ground-water rich in soluble salts, including sodium, the exchange positions become dominated with sodium ions. The last condition is found in the semi-desert and desert areas of the world where salt and sodium-saturated soils limit agricultural production. Physiologically, plant growth is limited by salt in the soil and also by its poor physical conditions. Clays which are saturated with calcium and hydrogen ions are stable and the soil crumbs are flocculated, whereas with sodium as the predominant ion the clay particles are dispersed and the soil becomes structureless and difficult to cultivate.

2.7 Diagrammatic representation of a clay-humus micelle with the adsorbed ions of hydrogen (H^+), calcium (Ca^{++}) and plant nutrients (K^+) etc.

Soil structure

Soil structure is an important physical characteristic of any soil. Structure in a soil is brought about by the individual particles of sand, silt or clay aggregating together in larger units known as *peds*. Soil structure is encouraged by the incorporation of organic matter, the gums and mucilages formed in the bacterial breakdown of organic matter help to bind the peds together. The peds have been described as the 'architecture' of the soil, and the spaces around them act as channels to conduct water through the soil. The spaces between the peds are also important for the soil microfauna which live in them. In fact the volume of the spaces in an organic-rich, medium-textured soil can be as high as 60 per cent in the topsoil, but is usually around 50 per cent. Cultivation reduces the number of the larger pores which are valuable for the movement of air and water through the soil. An average figure of 45 per cent is quoted for nineteen cultivated Georgia soils, with 57 per cent pore space in neighbouring uncultivated soils.

Soil structure readily falls into five categories: *structureless*, *platy* structures, *crumb* structures, *blocky* structures and *prismatic* structures. Structure is described according to the type, size and how well-formed the structures are in a soil. The different types of structure are described in Table 2.2 and depicted in Fig. 2.8. Maintenance of soil structure is important for agriculturalists the world over, for unless a soil is well-structured, crop yields are depressed, and soils are more liable to erosion. Structure can be weakened by over-cropping, or by the action of heavy machinery passing over the soil.

Soil air and water

The atmosphere penetrates down into the soil along the fissures and pores between the soil structures. The soil atmosphere is a natural continuation of the atmosphere above the soil, but, although it is similar in some respects, it differs in others. Compared with atmospheric air, soil air is usually saturated with water vapour and is richer in carbon dioxide.

Average composition of soil air
(per cent by volume)

	Oxygen	Carbon dioxide	Nitrogen
Soil air.	20.65	0.25	79.20
Atmospheric air	20.97	0.03	79.00

In the figures given above, the soil air has slightly less oxygen and more carbon dioxide, but the amounts of both these gases vary considerably according to the activity of the microorganisms living in the soil. Additions of leaf litter or organic manure greatly stimulate the bacterial activity which results in a depletion of oxygen in the soil air and an increase in the amount of carbon dioxide. The exchange of oxygen and carbon dioxide with the atmosphere takes place by diffusion, a process which is hindered if the soil pores and fissures are small and limited in number. If the pores and fissures are filled with water, fresh oxygen cannot easily diffuse in and such oxygen as may be present is soon used so that anaerobic conditions are produced. It is in these conditions that the growth of

2.8 Soil structures formed by the aggregation of the sand, silt and clay particles: (a) prismatic; (b) columnar; (c) angular blocky; (e) platy; (f) crumb or granular

a b c d e f

Table 2.2 Types and classes of soil structures

Class	Platelike with one dimension (the vertical) limited and greatly less than the other two; arranged around a horizontal plane; faces mostly horizontal	Prismlike with two dimensions (the horizontal) limited and considerably less than the vertical; arranged around a vertical line; vertical faces well defined; vertical angular.		Blocklike; polyhedronlike, or spheroidal, with three dimensions of the same order of magnitude, arranged around a point			
				Blocklike; blocks or polyhedrons having plane or curved surfaces that are casts of the moulds formed by the surrounding peds		Spheroids or polyhedrons having plane or curved surfaces which have slight or no accommodation to the faces of surrounding peds	
		Without rounded caps	With rounded caps	Faces flattened; most vertices sharply angular	Mixed rounded and flattened faces with many rounded vertices	Relatively non-porous peds	Porous peds
	Platy	Prismatic	Columnar	(Angular) Blocky[1]	Sub-angular Blocky[2]	Granular	Crumb
Very fine or very thin	Very thin platy; <1 mm.	Very fine prismatic; <10 mm.	Very fine columnar; <10 mm.	Very fine angular blocky; <5 mm.	Very fine sub-angular blocky; <5 mm.	Very fine granular; <1 mm.	Very fine crumb; <1 mm.
Fine or thin	Thin platy; 1 to 2 mm.	Fine prismatic; 10 to 20 mm.	Fine columnar; 10 to 20 mm.	Fine angular blocky; 5 to 10 mm.	Fine subangular blocky; 5 to 10 mm.	Fine granular; 1 to 2 mm.	Fine crumb; 1 to 2 mm.
Medium	Medium platy; 2 to 5 mm.	Medium prismatic; 20 to 50 mm.	Medium columnar; 20 to 50 mm.	Medium angular blocky; 10 to 20 mm.	Medium sub-angular blocky; 10 to 20 mm.	Medium granular; 2 to 5 mm.	Medium crumb; 2 to 5 mm.
Coarse or thick	Thick platy; 5 to 10 mm.	Coarse prismatic; 50 to 100 mm.	Coarse columnar; 50 to 100 mm.	Coarse angular blocky; 20 to 50 mm.	Coarse sub-angular blocky; 20 to 50 mm.	Coarse granular; 5 to 10 mm.	
Very coarse or very thick	Very thick platy; >10 mm.	Very coarse prismatic; >100 mm.	Very coarse columnar; >100 mm.	Very coarse angular blocky; >50 mm.	Very coarse sub-angular blocky; >50 mm.	Very coarse granular; >10 mm.	

[1] Sometimes called nut. The word 'angular' in the name can ordinarily be omitted.
[2] Sometimes called nuciform, nut, or sub-angular nut. Since the size connotation of these terms is a source of great confusion to many, they are not recommended.

most plants is inhibited and the process known as *gleying* is brought about.

The presence of air and water in the soil is almost complementary, for if the soil is saturated with water the air is driven out. In a saturated soil almost all the pore spaces and fissures between the peds are occupied by water. If the soil is allowed to drain so that all the water contained in the larger pores and cavities is removed, the water which is lost is known as *gravitational water*. About two days after flooding or heavy rain, a freely drained soil has lost its gravitational water and is said to be at *field capacity*. In this state, considerable amounts of water are still held in the finer pores and by capillary attraction. If the soil continues to lose moisture from these reserves of capillary water, the situation is reached where plants cannot obtain enough water to continue transpiration. Wilting then takes place from which the plant does not recover, this is the *permanent wilting point*. This point is not fixed and will vary according to the soil and plant concerned, for example some desert plants can obtain water from the soil against strong capillary forces, whereas a hydrophilic plant soon succumbs to dry conditions. The amount of water held in the soil between field capacity and permanent wilting point is referred to as the *available water capacity*. This amount will vary according to the texture and structure of the soil and is vitally important when considering the capability of a soil to supply a growing crop with its moisture requirements.

Further amounts of water can be obtained from soil in the laboratory. It is possible to bring the soil to air-dry conditions, but as this is a rather variable state, depending upon the humidity of the atmosphere, an oven-dry basis is used for most laboratory determinations. Water held at temperatures from air-dry up to oven-dry (105°C) is largely unavailable to plants. This water, and that released on drying in a muffle furnace at temperatures of 850°C can be regarded as part of the structure of the constituent minerals and is referred to as *hygroscopic water* (Fig. 2.9).

Water movement in soils can take place through the soil pores by saturated flow in which the rain or irrigation water infiltrates at the surface and continues to percolate downwards by gravity and by capillary forces. In unsaturated soils the movement is much restricted, taking place slowly in response to the capillary forces. Because of the variation of size of the pores and also the entrapped air, the capillary rise is not so great as it might be in a true capillary tube. Thus the rise of water from a water-table to the surface is probably limited to about a metre at the most. Water can also move in the vapour phase from a warmed soil layer into a cooler layer where condensation takes place. This form of movement is not so important, except possibly in desert soils, as the movement by gravitation and capillarity. The moisture regime of soils can be demonstrated simply by drilling a 10 cm. auger hole to different depths in the soil lining the hole with porous tiles and allowing the water-level to come to equilibrium. Observation at suitable intervals throughout the year will indicate the variation in level of water in the soil. Soil permeability can be measured by the rapidity with which the water-level returns following removal of water from the hole.

The soil water will dissolve any soluble constituents which may be present and as such contribute to the *soil solution* which is the medium whereby plants are supplied with nutrients. As has already been observed, inorganic salts dissociate into ions in solution. Many of these ions are attracted and adsorbed to the clay-humus micelles, but an equilibrium is reached so that there is a relationship between the numbers in the exchange positions and the ions still in the soil solution. In the case of the hydrogen ions, their concentration in solution is

2.9 Soil water. The width of a film of moisture around a solid soil particle determines the tension at which it is held. Represented in atmospheres, this tension holds water loosely at its outer edges, but as the water film is narrowed by drying, it becomes progressively more tightly held

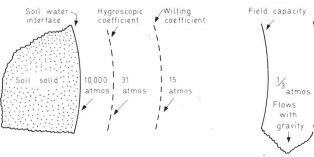

indicated by the pH scale in which neutrality is at pH 7. Values below pH 7 are acid and above pH 7 are alkaline. The average pH range of soils is from below pH 3 to pH 10, but in humid regions the normal range is from pH 5 to pH 7, and in arid regions it is from pH 7 to pH 9. Acid sulphate soils may reach pH 2, whereas at the other end of the scale, alkaline mineral soils may reach a pH value of 10.

Soil pH represents an easily determined feature of a soil, and one which has a general usefulness. Because several plant nutrients become less available to plants at the extremes of pH values and other elements become available in toxic amounts, the pH value is often a guide in the diagnosis of fertility problems. Soil pH values are also used in the classification of soils as can be seen in Chapter 5.

The removal of constituents from one horizon, their transport and eventual redeposition in another takes place through the medium of the soil solution. Normally, in humid climates, this movement will be downwards from the upper eluvial horizons into lower illuvial horizons of the profile. In arid climates, especially where groundwater is at shallow depth, movement can take place upwards as moisture is evaporated and salts left in the soil. Constituents will be taken into true solution if they are soluble, but removal can occur in colloidal form as in the case of clay and organic particles. Movement is also facilitated by chemical linkage such as iron with organic matter. Any soil constituents which are washed right through the profile and into the drains or to the water-table are lost from the soil system (Fig. 3.6).

3 FACTORS OF SOIL FORMATION

The consideration of how a soil forms inevitably leads to the question of the environmental controls affecting the manner in which a soil develops. The famous Russian soil scientist Dokuchaiev suggested five soil formers which controlled soil formation. These were: *parent material, climate, age of land, plant and animal organisms, topography*. In other words, the parent material is acted upon by the climate and the organisms, over a period of time, signified by the age of the land. Topography was considered also as it has much to do with water relationships. In more recent years, an American soil scientist, Jenny, considered similar soil-forming factors, and went on to show how they were functionally related in a form of an equation,

$$s = f'(Cl, O, R, P, T)$$

in which s, a soil property, is dependent upon (or is a function of) the soil-forming factors climate (Cl), organisms (O), relief (R), parent material (P) and time (T). The usefulness of this approach is that it is possible to take any soil-forming factor and consider its variations against the background of the others, thus examining the effect of that particular one. In view of the importance of these soil-forming factors a brief discussion of their individual roles in soil formation will be considered.

Climate
Climate is a composite concept which includes temperature, humidity, evapotranspiration as well as the type and amount of rainfall, duration of sunshine and many other variables. There is considerable range in world figures: rainfall for example varying from less than 250 mm. per annum to more than 12,500 mm. per annum and annual temperatures which range through 43 °C as well as those which range by only 0.5 or 1.0 °C. However, the annual figures themselves are not very suitable for a classification system. It is more important to assess the effect of seasonal variation as in the steppes and savanna lands, or the intensity of the rainfall e.g. as torrential downpours or as a gentle drizzle. These, as well as the local microclimatic effects, are most important but are unfortunately not often recorded. The rainfall which eventually penetrates into the soil is that which remains after losses by run-off and evaporation direct from the vegetation. Thus the moisture which enters the soil is less than the rainfall. It is further diminished by losses incurred by evapotranspiration from the soil surface and from moisture taken up by roots and transpired from the leaf surfaces of plants (Fig. 3.1). A number of attempts have been made to reduce the effects of rainfall and evapotranspiration to a single figure. Each has its merits, but lacks a world-wide signi-

3.1 Water entering the soil is not the same as the rainfall; the diagram shows the losses incurred before the water reaches the soil. Some water may be received by movement downslope through the soil

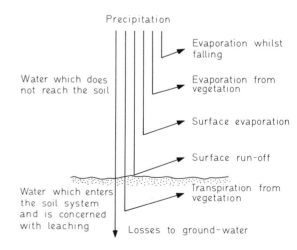

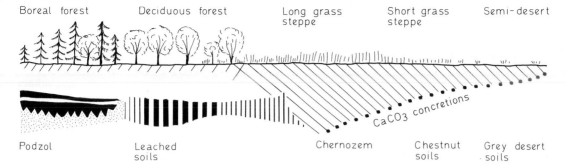

Boreal forest   Deciduous forest   Long grass steppe   Short grass steppe   Semi-desert

CaCO3 concretions

Podzol   Leached soils   Chernozem   Chestnut soils   Grey desert soils

3.2 The amount of rainfall can be broadly correlated with the depth to which calcium carbonate is leached. Thus it is completely removed in the podzol and brown earth and can appear on the surface of a desert soil

ficance. Thornthwaite's precipitation: effectiveness index works well in North America, but is less accurate in its assessment of the climate of Europe to quote but one example. It is possible to show correlations with rainfall for a number of different soil characteristics. One obvious example is the leaching of calcium carbonate from soil; the greater the rainfall the deeper the horizon of calcium carbonate appears in the soil until it is leached right out (Fig. 3.2). Clay type and content in soils is also slightly correlated with rainfall.

Temperature at first sight may not seem to have such an important role to play, but following an idea of Ramann, it is possible to show how it can be important over a long period of time.

In the table below the relative dissociation of water is taken as an index of the rate of chemical activity, and this, multiplied by the length of the weathering period, gives the absolute weathering factor. It can be seen that in tropical regions the effectiveness of weathering is almost ten times that of arctic regions and more than three times that of temperate regions. In tropical regions there is the additional fact that weathering has not been interrupted by a change in climate as in the glacial periods of higher latitudes. Therefore, deeper weathering is characteristic of the tropical

regions of the world. Up to 50 m. of weathered mantle often occur though depths are very variable. Correlations show an increase in clay content occurring with an increase of temperature. The increased rate of chemical activity described above is seen also in the organic decomposition of plant litter which is more rapid in tropical soils.

Organisms

The role of organisms in soil formation is of critical importance for without life there can be no soil formation. Bacteria and fungi are both responsible for the initial breakdown of plant tissue upon and within the soil surface. Various soil arthropods take the breakdown a stage further by eating through the plant remains. Mites (*Arachnidae*) and springtails (*Colembollae*) are chiefly responsible for this (Fig. 3.3). Incorporation of the organic matter into the mineral soil and the intimate association of the mineral and organic constituents are accomplished by earthworms or by termites.

Although the vegetation is dependent in the last instance upon the climate, it can also function as an independent variable. For example where coniferous plantations have replaced deciduous trees, podzols have formed, and where oak woodlands have developed on chernozems, leaching

	Average soil temperature	Relative dissociation of water	Days weathering	Weathering factor	
				Absolute	Relative
Arctic	10	1.7	100	170	1
Temperate	18	2.4	200	480	2.8
Tropical	34	4.5	360	1620	9.5

(From H. Jenny)

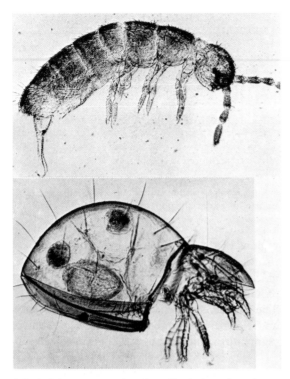

3.3 Soil fauna: examples of a collembola and a mite

3.4 The effect of aspect and relief: (a) soils on shady and sunny slopes; (b) normal, receiving and shedding sites

a. SHADED SLOPES

Colder soils
Wetter soils
Restricted soil fauna
Surface accumulation
of acid organic
matter

SUN-FACING SLOPES

Warmer soils
Drier soils
Varied soil fauna
Organic matter
incorporated

Sun's rays

Shaded slope

Sunny slope

b. Rainfall

Rainfall

Run-off

Less leaching on hill

Run-off

Increased leaching in hollow

Normal site   Receiving site   Shedding site

has been encouraged. Much greater changes occur when forest is cleared for agricultural development. The supply of organic matter is interrupted and changed; plant nutrients originally circulating in the soil–plant system are taken out in the form of crops, and others are added in the form of fertiliser applications. The whole soil environment can be changed by the addition of lime to raise the pH value. The installation of a drainage system changes the hydrological relationships while cultivation mixes horizons previously distinct. The activity of man considerably affects soil development.

Relief

The effect of relief upon climate is well known for its depression of temperature and increase in rainfall. However, associated with upland areas is a greater incidence of cloudiness and hence less solar warming; evapotranspiration is also reduced leading to conditions favouring the development of thicker organic horizons. Such conditions are particularly prevalent in the northern and western parts of the British Isles. The aspect of slopes can greatly affect the amount of solar warming, so that different soils will form on sun-facing slopes as compared with shady slopes (Fig. 3.4). Where very steep slopes occur, the rate of erosion may mean that a mature soil profile does not have a chance to form, accordingly some soil classification distinguish a group of mountain soils. Although not so obviously seen in the British environment, it is possible for the transfer of soil constituents to take place downslope. This migration of material brings about the relationship of soils to their position on the landscape. This interrelationship is known as a *catena* (pp. 49, 101).

Parent material

The parent material is described by Jenny as 'the initial state of the soil system', but it is more generally described as the consolidated or unconsolidated material little affected by the present weathering cycle from which the soil has developed. The more simple definition that it is 'that which lies beneath the true soil horizons' could be misleading, as many soils have developed from diverse parent materials of differing origins, and not simply from the rock beneath them. For example a soil can develop in a glacial drift or *loess* overlying an unweathered rock which is unaffected by the current processes of soil formation. If the cover of superficial material is thin, then the soil can be developed in both it and the bedrock beneath.

It is useful at this point to distinguish between weathering and soil forming processes, the former is a geological process, and the latter a pedological process (see p. 30). In addition to physical breakdown, weathering includes the geo-chemical processes of solution, hydrolysis, carbonization, oxidation and reduction as well as the rearrangement of the structure of clay minerals and the formation of new ones. Soil-forming processes are considered in the next chapter. Weathering and soil-forming processes can carry on either separately or together. In an old soil, weathering will occur at depth below the genetic soil horizons which have formed near the surface, and in a young soil which is shallow the two processes can operate within the same few centimetres of soil.

In most environments the balance of soil-forming factors is such that different rocks when weathered will give rise to different soil types because of their mineral composition. This has been demonstrated in Scotland, where brown earths form on basic igneous rocks and podzols form on acid igneous rocks under identical weathering conditions. The differences between soils developed over calcareous and non-calcareous parent materials are recognised in many soil classifications. The presence in these soils of large quantities of calcium causes the flocculation of iron, aluminium and humus thus inhibiting movement and retarding the formation of a mature soil profile. In Wales, outcrops of the Carboniferous Limestone on Black Mountain, Dyfed give rise to the development of brown earths at an elevation and under a rainfall which ensures peaty gleys and peaty gley podzols on non-calcareous parent materials. Similarly, in the Peak District of Derbyshire, the limestones have a cover of brown earths whereas adjacent sandstones and shales only support moorland with peaty gleys and peaty gley podzols.

Extremely porous sandy parent materials rapidly achieve a mature profile because materials in solution or suspension move through them easily. Thus, many sandy parent materials throughout the geological succession develop acid brown soils, brown podzolic soils or podzols. Podzols are found especially on the coarse-textured glacio-fluvial sands and gravels, as well as on the sandstones of the Tertiary formations in the London and Hampshire basins. Brown podzolic soils are commonly found to occur on steeply sloping sites in Wales and Scotland where they are developed from Lower Palaeozoic strata.

In contrast, clay soils with slow drainage do not form zonal profile characteristics so quickly, and in any case are influenced by gleying. Wide expanses of boulder clays in the lowlands of England have surface-water gley soils and in the uplands these also develop peatyness and support peaty gleys. Alluvial materials are frequently well-sorted, often are silty and possess organic matter in quantity to greater depths than other soils. Accumulation of organic matter may be associated with alluvial material giving, when drained, highly fertile fen peat soils.

In the sub-humid and semi-arid lands conditions are suitable for the development of soils rich in montmorillonitic clays. Parent materials with these dark-coloured and deeply cracking soils are of considerable interest and are discussed under the heading of vertisols (p. 86). In the humid tropics soils developed upon basaltic parent materials have special properties which result in the strong adsorption of iron and phosphate in spite of the strong leaching experienced which has converted adjacent soils into Ferrallitic or Ferruginous soils (see pp. 82 and 84).

Where marshes are drained, where sand, loess or volcanic ash accumulates or where land is completely disrupted by opencast mining, new parent materials are exposed for the processes of soil formation to work upon. In all other cases the soils themselves may be changed gradually should the other factors of soil formation alter in direction or magnitude.

Time
Soils, like organisms and landscapes, develop with the passage of time and gradually attain features of maturity. Young soils retain many features of the parent material from which they were developed, but as they become older they acquire features: the addition of organic matter, and the development and increasing clarity of horizons.

27

When the soil has reached the point at which it is at equilibrium with its environment it can be considered to be a *mature* soil. Most early forms of soil classifications are based on the characters of the mature soil profile.

There are several examples of the formation of soils which can be said to have taken place for a definite number of years. Often these examples are related to catastrophic events like the eruption of Krakatoa in 1883, or to the development of soils on landslides and earthflows. The retreat of glaciers has left behind an expanse of parent material upon which soil formation has begun. As records have been kept of the former positions of glacier snouts it is possible to date the beginning of soil formation accurately. Archaeological monuments can effectively arrest soil development below their sites and give an indication of the rapidity of soil change. Evidence from Britain shows that brown soils, present in Neolithic times, became brown podzolic soils by the Bronze Age and podzols in Iron Age and Roman times.

The draining of a lake exposes its floor to the processes of soil formation. The draining of the Ijsselmeer polders has provided much interesting information upon what the Dutch call the '*ripening*' of soils. The development of series of parallel dunes has again given some indication of the rate at which soils develop. An examination of the soils which are developing upon mining spoil heaps shows sequences of maturity related to the amount of time which has elapsed since the material was dumped.

Where older soils occur, as in the tropical regions, it is possible to establish a sequence of soil maturity correlated with the morphology of the landscape thus linking together two branches of geographical study. The position of the soil on the landscape gives its age relationships (Fig. 3.5). In this case the time sequence of the geomorphologist is similar to that of the pedologist though, for most soils, the period of formation is shorter. In the British Isles it is generally considered that soil formation dates from the end of the Pleistocene glaciations about 10,000 years ago. Most soils formed in the previous interglacial periods were eroded away, but pockets of deeper weathered material in Scotland and South Wales indicate that a former period of soil formation took place in the warmer climate of interglacial times. Changes of climate are known to have occurred since, and following the Iron Age period of British history increased podzolisation occurred in southern Britain. Many profiles have features which suggest that the present soil-forming factors have changed slightly. Lower horizons, which bear the imprint of different conditions, have yet to be brought into equilibrium with the present environment.

The soil as a system
The functional relationship of the soil-forming factors shown by Jenny is an extremely useful approach to the study of soils and his book represents a milestone in pedological research. However, there are some real difficulties in applying this approach in every case. The problems of giving climate, organisms or parent material a value which can be substituted in the equation are large and can only be resolved by the use of subjective decisions. Furthermore, it is almost impossible to isolate completely the variables; relief and climate are often closely related and with them the nature of the vegetative cover.

A possible means of overcoming some of these difficulties is by the use of systems analysis. In Chapter 1 the idea of the soil as a system was

3.5 Age and position of soil on landscape. Different geomorphic surfaces give rise to a sequence of younger, mature and relic soils in certain parts of the world

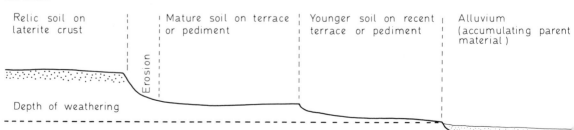

Relic soil on laterite crust

Mature soil on terrace or pediment

Younger soil on recent terrace or pediment

Alluvium (accumulating parent material)

Erosion

Depth of weathering

introduced and it was stated that various inputs and outputs occurred associated with biological, hydrological and geochemical cycles (Fig. 3.6). Weathering of the rocks produces an input which becomes part of the soil, some of the elements released will be plant nutrients and these become an output of the soil system and an input of the biological cycle. In this case, some recycling will occur when nutrients are returned in the plant litter at the end of the season. Losses occur when dissolved minerals and nutrients are carried away in the drainage water. An advantage of the systems approach lies in the use of feed-back mechanisms and recycling which help to regulate and maintain the mature soil. Within the soil profile minerals may be transformed or reconstituted from elements or compounds leached from elsewhere and iron clay, humus or salts may be translocated from one horizon to another. Most soils are in a state of slow evolution in response to changes in the factors controlling their development, but some of the oldest tropical soils may well approximate to the steady state or dynamic equilibrium advocated by system theorists.

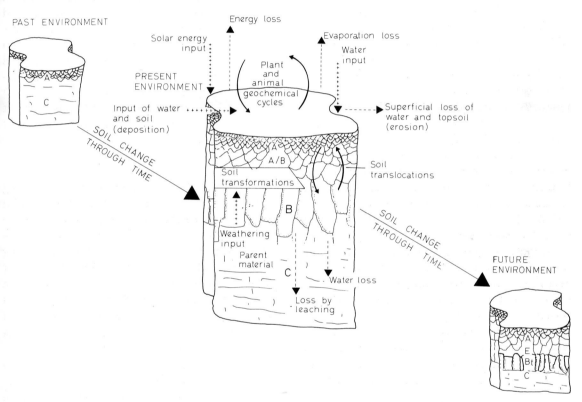

3.6 The soil as an open system. A soil area, or pedon, is shown as part of a system evolving through time. Profile characteristics result from additions (inputs) and losses (outputs) as well as translocations and transformations within the profile.

4 PROCESSES OF SOIL FORMATION

The processes of soil formation are those which modify the regolith and give it the acquired characteristics which distinguish soil from parent material. These processes are weathering, leaching, eluviation, podzolization, rubefaction, calcification, ferrallitization, salinization, alkalization, solodization, gleying, accumulation of organic matter and pedoturbation. These processes are not mutually exclusive: gleying and podzolization can be seen to take place simultaneously in humid regions of the world; gleying and salinization are frequently seen in low-lying areas of the semi-arid parts of the world.

Weathering

Weathering is an important precurser of soil development. Physical weathering is restricted mainly to arctic and desert regions, but chemical weathering is dominant in the production of parent materials elsewhere in the world. Rain water charged with acids derived from organic breakdown products and carbon dioxide forms a solution which attacks the unweathered material. In soils of the tropical regions weathering of the parent material frequently takes place far below the surface but weathering can operate also alongside the soil-forming processes in the soil horizons. This is particularly evident in shallow, immature soils where fragments of rock incorporated in the soil are in the process of weathering into parent material.

When soils are developing from freshly deposited alluvial material in marsh situations, either along rivers or on tidal saltings, the mixture of mineral and organic matter with water undergoes many physical, chemical and biological changes before it becomes a soil. These changes are collectively referred to as *ripening*.

Leaching

This is the term given to the process by which soluble constituents are removed from the soil. Where rainfall exceeds evaporation, readily soluble salts are dissolved by downward percolating water. Consequently, soluble salts are removed in the drainage water and do not persist in soils of humid regions. Over a long period of time, sparingly soluble materials such as calcium carbonate are removed from soils in humid regions. Leaching also attacks bases, such as calcium, potassium and magnesium, held as exchangeable ions by the

4.1 The process of leaching

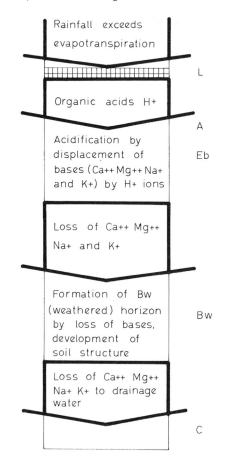

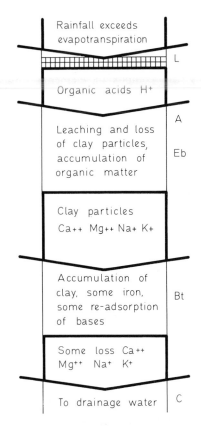

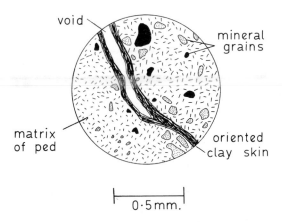

4.2 The process of eluviation

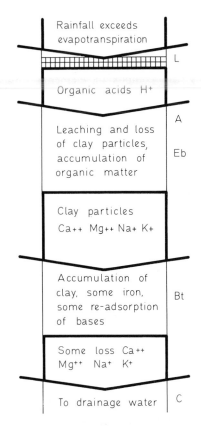

Diagram labels (left figure):
Rainfall exceeds evapotranspiration — L
Organic acids H⁺ — A
Leaching and loss of clay particles, accumulation of organic matter — Eb
Clay particles Ca₊₊ Mg₊₊ Na⁺ K⁺
Accumulation of clay, some iron, some re-adsorption of bases — Bt
Some loss Ca₊₊ Mg⁺⁺ Na⁺ K⁺
To drainage water — C

4.3 A thin section of soil as seen through a microscope showing an oriented clay skin lining the walls of a pore.

clay-humus complex and substitutes hydrogen ions in their place. Thus a major effect of leaching is gradually to make the soil more acid leading to the development of the *cambic* or 'weathered' B horizon (Fig. 4.1). After a prolonged period of leaching as in some soils of tropical regions, only quartz, kaolinite, hydrated iron oxides and some other very stable minerals remain in the soil. The leaching process is checked when soils are limed for agricultural purposes. Plants also tend to reduce the effects of leaching as they bring mineral elements from the subsoil to the surface where they are liberated by the death and decomposition of the plants.

Eluviation
In the past the term eluviation simply implied the removal of substances from the upper or eluvial horizons of a soil. Recently, it has become customary to distinguish between loss by solution

and eluviation, which refers specifically to the loss in suspension of material from a soil horizon. Finely dispersed humus and clay particles as well as other weathering products can move as colloidal suspensions from eluvial to illuvial soil horizons. This process appears to be encouraged by a climate in which a period of desiccation results in the soil shrinking and cracking so that on re-wetting mechanical eluviation down the cracks of clay or humus can occur.

One of the most important results is the development of a B horizon enriched in clay which is referred to as an *argillic* horizon, a Bt horizon or a 'textural B horizon' (Fig. 4.2). The clay content of the illuvial horizon can be increased considerably compared with the amount remaining in the E horizon of the same soil. The E horizon can be recognised by its paler colour and weaker structure. Unlike podzolization, where the clay particles are broken down, eluviation is regarded as a purely mechanical washing of particles suspended in the soil solution into the lower horizons of a soil. For this reason the process is frequently referred to by its French name of *lessivage* and the soils developed *sols lessivés*. In well developed examples, clay skins can be seen with the aid of a hand-lens or even with the naked eye (Figs. 4.3 and 4.4).

It is also possible to observe the movement of silt particles from the eluvial horizon of grey wooded soils in Canada and the derno-podzolic

31

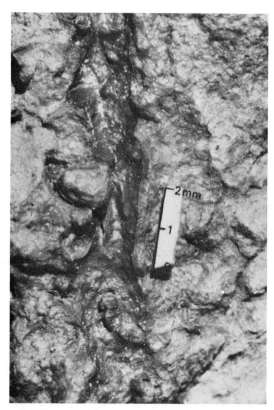

4.4 Thick clay skin in pore and thin clay skins on ped surface

from the plants, percolates through the mor humus and enters the mineral soil. This solution is capable of causing the breakdown of clay minerals by disruption of the mineral structure, releasing the component elements. Silica and aluminium, together with iron, which forms complexes with organic substances, are said to be mobilized and removed from the surface horizons as the solutions percolate downwards (Fig. 4.5).

There is therefore a tendency for quartz silica to accumulate in the immediate sub-surface of the soil forming the characteristic bleached grey horizon of a podzol. This is a relative accumulation though, as in the presence of organic matter, some silica is reported to be lost as well. This light-coloured eluvial horizon which has lost constituents is described as an Ea horizon or *albic* horizon.

4.5 The process of podzolization

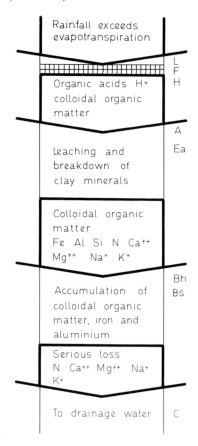

soils in U.S.S.R. This results in a characteristic white tonguing of the E horizon into the B horizon which is referred to by the term 'glossic'.

Podzolization

The process of podzolization is prevalent in the soils of the cool humid parts of the world and produces soils of the *podzolic group* and the *podzols* in particular. These two groups of soils can be differentiated because in the case of the development of podzols, the processes are more severe and the profile formed is more distinct both in appearance and in its physical and chemical properties. Characteristically, podzols are developed beneath heath or coniferous forest.

Podzolization involves the development of an extremely acid humus formation known as mor, in which the rate of decomposition of debris from plants such as heath or coniferous trees is slow, allowing litter, fermentation and humus layers to accumulate (Fig. 2.6). Rainwater falling on the vegetation acquires soluble breakdown substances

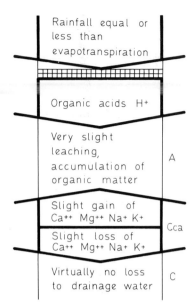

Rainfall equal or less than evapotranspiration

Organic acids H⁺

Very slight leaching, accumulation of organic matter | A

Slight gain of Ca⁺⁺ Mg⁺⁺ Na⁺ K⁺

Cca

Slight loss of Ca⁺⁺ Mg⁺⁺ Na⁺ K⁺

Virtually no loss to drainage water | C

4.6 The process of calcification

The iron oxides which are mobilised from the surfaces of the mineral soil particles in the eluvial horizon, together with the aluminium and organic matter, are eventually deposited in the illuvial horizons. There are several different opinions as to the reason for the deposition of material in the B horizon lower in the profile. These explanations include wetting and drying cycles, changes in the pH value, presence of flocculating ions and the breaking down of the iron-humus bonds by ageing or by bacterial attack. The formation of these illuvial horizons constitutes the *spodic* horizon of U.S. Soil Taxonomy or the *'podzolic'* horizon of the recently adopted classification in England and Wales.

Strongly acid conditions developed in all podzols limit the range of soil fauna present; in particular earthworms are usually absent. The soil undergoes little mixing by faunal pedoturbation and so the pronounced horizons of the podzol profile are allowed to develop.

Calcification

The process of calcification is characteristic of low-rainfall areas in continental interior situations. Leaching is slight and although downward movement does take place, the soluble constituents are not removed from the soil profile. These soils are only wetted to a depth of between

1 m. and 1.5 m. when the moisture begins to re-evaporate (Fig. 4.6). A *calcic* horizon of calcium carbonate accumulates in the B or upper C horizon where the impetus of the downward percolating rain water (or snow melt) is lost. As these soils are relatively unleached, the exchange capacity is dominated with calcium ions, and to a lesser extent with magnesium ions. The presence of these ions has a stabilising effect upon the colloids and movement in the soil is inhibited.

The type of humus is mull, produced by the natural vegetation of grasses. These grasses have intensive root systems which when dead provide large amounts of organic matter to the soil. The aerial parts of the plant also return bases to the soil surface. Winter frost and summer drought combine to limit the rate of decomposition so that over many years a very rich and deep A horizon accumulates.

Rubefaction

Rather different conditions obtain where there is a marked dry season as in some of the tropical savannas and sub-tropical regions subjected to strong summer drought. The soil is progressively desiccated during the dry season and in the rainy season it is leached. Carbonates are removed from the soil and eluviation of clay occurs when the soil is re-wetted at the end of the dry season. The dehydration experienced by the soil results in the transformation of hydrated ferric oxides into haematite. This gives the soil a bright red colour, the development of which is called rubefaction. Frequently, the eluviated clay and the iron oxides are associated in an argillic horizon in the red Mediterranean soils or tropical ferrallitic soils.

Ferrallitization

The process of ferrallitization is characteristic of soil formation in the humid tropical regions of the world. In the past this process has been referred to as laterization, latosolization or kaolinization; these terms have become confused in their definition and use, so the term ferrallitization is preferable. In simple terms this process involves the relative accumulation of sesquioxides of iron and aluminium with the loss of silica. Prolonged exposure to the humid tropical environment produces a highly weathered, low base-status *oxic* horizon. The process of ferrallitization is accompanied by strong leaching of the soil, so the pH values are low. The rapid decay and re-cycling of the elements contained in the leaf fall from the tropical rain forest keep bases and nutrients in rapid circulation between plant and soil. Clay formation is restricted to the kaolinite group of clays which are frequently associated with iron as a cement. The resulting soil material is usually freely drained, red in colour and does not disperse easily in water (Fig. 4.7).

Salinization

In arid climates the rainfall is irregular and insufficient to remove soluble salts from the soil, although in semi-arid areas there is a redistribution of the salts into the lower parts of the landscape. The occurrence of soils affected by salt is associated with the soils which have imperfect or poor natural drainage. Frequently these areas are the alluvial plains and other areas which otherwise would be able to produce considerably greater yields of crops.

The enrichment of a soil with salt is the process of salinization. This is usually achieved by the evaporation of moisture from the surface of the soil. Salts in solution are drawn upwards by capillary action and then are deposited as the water is evaporated. As a result, these soils develop a surface encrustation of salt and are known as *white alkali* or *solonchak* soils (Fig. 4.8). Such soils possess *salic* horizons. Salt can be derived from a salt-rich geological substratum, or it can be derived from salt sea-spray blown inland which gradually accumulates in the unleached soils of the arid and semi-arid areas.

These soils are called primary saline soils. The use of water containing even small quantities of soluble salts can result in salinization of soils in irrigation schemes in hot dry countries. The resulting soils are referred to as secondary saline soils as they only occur through human interference in the natural environment. In both primary and secondary saline soils the depth to the water table in the soil is of critical importance.

Alkalization

The process of alkalization occurs when sodium ions dominate the exchange positions of the clay-humus complex. This is achieved when slight leaching removes the soluble salts. As the solubil-

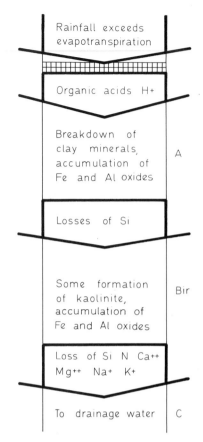

4.7 The process of ferratillization

ities of calcium and magnesium are lower than that of sodium it remains in the soil solution after the divalent ions of calcium and magnesium have been precipitated. Drying can also concentrate the amount of sodium ions remaining and they attach and monopolise the exchange positions on the clay-humus complex giving the soil a *natric* horizon, and a *black alkali* or *solonetz* soil results (Fig. 4.9).

Solodization

The process of solodization or removal of sodium ions from the clay-humus complex, results in a range of soils from the *solodized solonetz* to the *solod*. The solod is largely leached of metal cations and is dominated with hydrogen ions, resulting in an acid soil.

Gleying

The presence of water in a soil for long periods brings about anaerobic conditions as has been

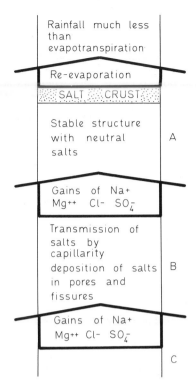

4.8 The process of salinization

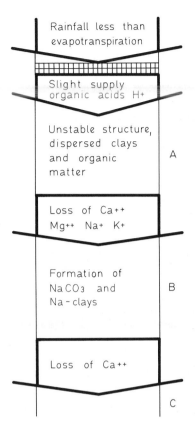

4.9 The process of alkalization

explained in Chapter 2. As this can happen in almost all environments, the process of gleying produces features which enable the pedologist to group these soils together as *hydromorphic* soils which are considered to be intrazonal in their world distribution (Chapter 10). These poorly drained soils frequently occur on plateau sites or on the lower parts of the landscape, and often are developed from parent materials similar to those of adjacent freely drained soils.

The process of gleying involves the reduction of iron compounds and either their removal from the profile or their segregation into mottles or concretions. Usually the gleying process is accomplished with saturated conditions in the presence of bacteria and organic matter. The metabolic activity of the bacteria is responsible for the oxygen deficit, and reducing conditions develop best where the soil solution is stagnant. Exposure of the soil to the open air allows re-oxygenation to take place and colour changes occur. The colour of a strongly gleyed soil or gleyed horizon may frequently be an unrelieved grey or bluish colour, but where some oxygena-

tion takes place, there will be mottles of rust-coloured ferric oxide.

Two basic types of gley soil are recognised. Where an impervious horizon occurs within the soil profile a *surface-water gley* results, and where water rises up in the soil from an impervious horizon beneath the soil, a *ground-water gley* is produced. It is usual to find ground-water gley soils in areas which receive an inflow of surface and ground water. In this case, the soil must be permeable if water rising between the grains or peds is to saturate the lower soil horizons. With anaerobic conditions the decomposition of plant residues on the surface is slow and peat frequently accumulates on soils with a high level of ground-water. The colour of these soils is frequently an unrelieved grey of ferrous iron, or, if the soil dries occasionally, there may be a few mottles of rust-coloured ferric oxide. Surface-water gley soils can occur almost anywhere on the landscape where an impermeable horizon such as a Bt horizon prevents the downward passage of water through the profile. Localised gleying results, particularly on the faces and pores of the peds which become grey coloured. The ped interiors, in contrast, retain the brighter colours of ferric iron giving an overall impression of mottling when revealed in a section. This soil closely resembles the *pseudogley* described by European authors.

Accumulation of organic matter

When plant debris falls onto the soil surface it can accumulate to form a litter layer. However, in most soils the process of *humification* begins with the breakdown of vegetable debris which eventually results in the formation of humus, a black or dark brown amorphous material. In strongly acid soils such as podzols, accumulation of humus can occur on the soil surface but generally it is incorporated into the soil, especially the A horizon, by the activity of the soil fauna. The effect of adding organic matter to the soil is to darken its colour, a process known as *melanization*.

In conditions of very poor soil drainage *peat formation* is encouraged in association with the gley soils present. Basically there are two types of peat, the moor peat which is acid, and the fen peat which is neutral or mildly alkaline. Further subdivision can be made upon botanical composition, structure and degree of decomposition. The characteristics of these two basic forms result from the way in which they have developed. The acid moor peat develops on upland areas where high rainfall results in the leaching of all bases so that acid conditions set in and there is very slow decomposition of the plant debris. In certain areas deep peat has accumulated to depths of 3–5 m.

Raised bogs occur in sites where an acid peat sustained from the nutrient supplies of the rainwater overlies a peat formed in a declivity of the landscape. The true fen peats developed in waters liberally supplied with bases and are neutral or mildly alkaline in reaction. When adequately drained, the soils developed upon such deposits are usually very fertile with high land values as in the Fens of eastern England.

Pedoturbation

Where the supply of bases is plentiful in regions with a summer drought, as occurs in low-lying areas of the landscape, montmorillonitic clays are more likely to form and become the dominant clay mineral. The inherent swelling and shrinking properties of these clays introduce a process of pedoturbation in which the soil is continually mixed by expansion and contraction (see Vertisols, p. 86). In many soils mixing by soil-living fauna is an important feature of their development and this process is referred to as faunal pedoturbation. Freeze–thaw cycles can be responsible for soil mixing especially in soils of the tundra regions. In regions which experience strong winds, soils are mixed when trees are blown over and the roots torn from the ground.

5 SOIL CLASSIFICATION

Classification is only a contrivance to order a subject, perhaps to understand and remember its content more easily, certainly to show how one part is related to the whole. A classification serves to make a basis from which further enquiry can proceed. As far as soils are concerned, classification is still developing, and numerous attempts have been made from different points of view to group soils into natural classes. However, a soil which in one place is extensive, elsewhere may only occupy a small and insignificant area, or may not be represented at all. It is in some ways unfortunate that all soil classifications are not marked 'provisional', because as more knowledge of the soil is collected, new groupings are deemed necessary and older ones may be redefined.

Although soil classification is fundamental to a study of World Soils, students new to the subject may find it more useful to return to this chapter after reading the book. For the time being, they are recommended to proceed to the simplified approach adopted specifically for this book which can be found on p. 46 and in Table 5.9.

Several recent attempts to classify soils are based upon the intrinsic properties of the soils, though in the past this has not always been the case. Many classifications have been based upon an interpretation and comparison of mature soils with attempts at grouping in a logical, natural system of categories. A *mature* soil can be described as one which is in dynamic equilibrium with its environment. A *young* soil is still in the process of adjustment to the current situation. Change of climate, cultivation, clearance of vegetation, lowering of ground-water, removal of salts can all result in readjustments being made in the soil with consequent modifications to the nature and appearance of the horizons present.

It is generally accepted that the impetus of present-day soil science began with V. V. Doku-chaiev in U.S.S.R. and E. W. Hilgard in U.S.A. Dokuchaiev is credited with producing the first natural soil classification, a classification based on observable features in the soil itself. He recognised that the soil was an independent natural body which could be studied by field and laboratory methods, based upon the interpretation of the morphology of the profile. It was observed by Dokuchaiev and his collaborators that many soil types had a definite geographical location, associated with definite climatic regions and vegetation types. This led to the development of the idea of zonal soils which is the main feature of the final classification produced by Dokuchaiev in 1900, and which still influences current world soil maps.

In Britain much interest in the soil was expressed by the various writers of the *General Views of Agriculture* of particular countries, commissioned at the end of the eighteenth century by the Board of Agriculture, though none of their work was systematic in its content or description. In the period from 1900 to 1914 a number of attempts at soil mapping were made and close relation was found with the drift maps of the Geological Survey. Fortunately it was appreciated that the correlation was not perfect, and in the years following the 1914–18 war visits by American soil surveyors, together with the appointment of soil survey assistants to the regional agricultural chemists led to the adoption of the American system of soil series, based upon the characters of the soil profile.

Much of the early work in soil survey in Britain was undertaken by Professor G. W. Robinson at Bangor. He produced a classification of world soils, but unfortunately did not make a classification of British soils, although he reviewed the present state of the knowledge of British soils at the time he wrote (Table 5.1).

Table 5.1   *Classification of world soils by G. W. Robinson (1947)*

	Completely leached (pedalfers)	Presence of raw humus	1. Humus podzols 2. Iron podzols
Soils with free drainage		Absence of raw humus	3. Brown earths 4. Degraded chernozems 5. Prairie soils 6. Yellow podzolic soils 7. Red podzolic soils 8. Tropical red loams 9. Ferrallites
	Incompletely leached (pedocals)		10. Chernozems 11. Chestnut soils 12. Brown desert soils 13. Grey desert soils
Soils with impeded drainage	Absence of soluble salts	Sub-arctic	14. Tundra
		Temperate	15. Gley soils 16. Gley podzols 17. Peat podzols 18. Peat soils
		Sub-tropical and tropical	19. Vlei soils
	Presence of soluble salts		20. Saline soils 21. Alkaline soils 22. Soloti soils

His classification reflected the approach of pedologists to the classification of world soils before and immediately after the 1939–45 war. It was based upon mature profiles and it included drainage, degree of leaching and type of humus in its criteria. For these it drew upon the experience of Marbut (1927) and subsequent modifications of his classification by the American Soil Survey. Robinson also foreshadowed ideas later expressed by Kubiena, whose system of classification has been most influential in Europe. Kubiena grouped profiles by their horizon sequence as designated by the horizon index letters, A, B, C, etc., whilst the type of humus played an important role in the second stage of his classification. With five basic groups: A(C), raw soils; AC, rankers and rendzinas; A(B)C, brown soils; ABC, podzols; and B/ABC, salt crust soils, this classification had the great merit of simplicity and illustrated the use of profile morphology in soil classification.

Kubiena's ideas have had considerable influence upon subsequent soil classification in Europe. Classification by degree of evolution of profile can now be seen in the French, Belgian,

German and British systems of classification. The study of humus form and the micromorphological structure of the soil are other aspects which Kubiena introduced into his classification which have since found much favour.

The classification evolved for France, and those countries with which France has close historical ties, has as its essential criteria the degree of evolution of the profile, types of clay minerals, presence of sesquioxides and the degree of modification from the parent material, the type of organic matter and the effects of gleying. There and twelve classes (Table 5.2).

Many of these soil groupings can be traced to those suggested by Kubiena in his 1953 system of classification, such as the degree of evolution of the profile and the degree of separation of the sesquioxides of iron and aluminium as well as the importance of the type of organic matter. Within each of the ten classes, subclasses are distinguished by different pedo-climatic conditions or other significant characters including base status in the Isohumic soils and the presence of clay illuviation in the sols lessivés compared with the sols bruns. Great groups are identified

Table 5.2 *Classes and subclasses of the classification used in France (Commission de Pedologie et de Cartographie des sols, 1967)*

I	*Raw mineral soils* (A)C profile without organic horizons	VII	*Brown soils* A(B)C or ABC profile with mull humus	
	1.1 non-climatic raw mineral soils		7.1 of humid temperate climates	
	1.2 arctic desert soils		7.2 of continental temperate climates	
	1.3 hot desert soils		7.3 of boreal climates	
			7.4 of tropical climates	

I   *Raw mineral soils* (A)C profile without organic horizons
    1.1   non-climatic raw mineral soils
    1.2   arctic desert soils
    1.3   hot desert soils

II   *Weakly developed soils* AC profile lacking in calcium
    2.1   with permafrost
    2.2   rankers
    2.3   grey sub-desert soils
    2.4   non-climatic weakly developed soils

III   *Vertisols* AC or A(B)C profile with expanding clays
    3.1   with reducing conditions and no external drainage
    3.2   with external drainage

IV   *Andosols* A(B)C profile with high exchange capacity derived from volcanic ash
    4.1   of cold climates
    4.2   of tropical climates

V   *Calcareous soils* AC or A(B)C profile derived from calcareous or gypsiferous parent materials
    5.1   Rendzinas
    5.2   Brown calcareous soils
    5.3   Gypsiferous soils

VI   *Isohumic soils* AC or A(B)C profile rich in well-humified organic matter
    6.1   of humid regions
    6.2   of cold regions
    6.3   of regions with rain in the cool season
    6.4   of regions with rain in the hot season

VII   *Brown soils* A(B)C or ABC profile with mull humus
    7.1   of humid temperate climates
    7.2   of continental temperate climates
    7.3   of boreal climates
    7.4   of tropical climates

VIII   *Podzols* ABC profile with mor humus
    8.1   of temperate climates
    8.2   of cold climates
    8.3   with gleying

IX   *Sesquioxide-rich soils* ABC profile with separation of iron oxides and medium to high exchange capacity
    9.1   ferruginous tropical soils
    9.2   red Mediterranean soils

X   *Ferrallitic soils* ABC profile with loss of silica and separation of the oxides of iron and aluminium
    10.1   weakly leached
    10.2   moderately leached
    10.3   strongly leached

XI   *Hydromorphic soils* profile with gleying and organic matter accummulation
    11.1   organic soils
    11.2   peaty mineral soils
    11.3   non-humic gley soils

XII   *Halomorphic soils* profile with soluble salts
    12.1   salic soils with stable structure
    12.2   sodic soils with unstable structure

by morphology and the intensity of the processes which produced the profile. Families include soils with similar lithological features and series are defined by a common detailed profile morphology.

The great trouble with most soil classifications is that they are produced for semi-natural and natural soils, whereas much of the landscape has been affected by the work of mankind. Certainly, it is possible to have different phases of the same soil series under natural conditions and under agricultural conditions, but most soil classifications especially at a national level are based upon the natural profile, developed under woodland or heath.

There are some properties of a soil which do not change materially with agricultural practice, and of these the texture is the most readily observed feature. Thus, a classification can be built up quite objectively upon soils with uniform textures U, soils with textures which gradually change from the surface to the parent material G, or soils which abruptly change in texture somewhere in the soil profile D. This system has been the basis of a classification and map of Australian soils by Northcote (1960) (Table 5.3).

39

Table 5.3 *Classification of Australian soils by Northcote (1960)*

I	Soils with uniform texture profiles U	
	Uc	coarse textures
	Um	medium textures
	Uf	fine textures
	Ug	fine textures showing cracking
II	Soils with gradational upland profiles G	
	Gc	soils calcareous throughout profile
	Gn	soils not calcareous throughout profile
III	Soils with contrasting (Duplex) texture profiles D	
	Dr	red clayey sub-soils
	Db	brown clayey sub-soils
	Dy	yellow clayey sub-soils
	Dd	dark clayey sub-soils
	Dg	gley clayey sub-soils
IV	Soils with organic profiles O	
	No further classification	

Other methods of soil classification are aimed at specific purposes. For example, in semi-arid areas where much work has been done on alluvial soils for irrigation projects, the presence or absence of salt is an important criterion in the classification. Most classifications include the acidity or alkalinity (pH value) of soils as a criterion at some stage.

As more knowledge has become available, it has been appreciated that it is sometimes difficult to classify soils in a rigid system because in nature they form a continuum with many gradations. To overcome some of the difficulties the American Soil Survey staff produced a new and comprehensive system of soil classification, published as *Soil Taxonomy* (1975). This avoids all the old colour names and folk names for soils, and new terms have been evolved to describe soils by diagnostic horizons. An *epipedon* is a surface horizon which is darkened by organic matter, and which includes the eluvial horizons. There are six of these horizons, briefly described as follows:

Mollic epipedon. A dark coloured, thick surface horizon, with over 50 per cent of the exchange capacity saturated by base cations.

Anthropic epipedon. Similar to a mollic epipedon but with a high amount of phosphate accumulated by long-continued farming.

Umbric epipedon. A dark surface horizon less than 50 per cent of the exchange capacity saturated by base cations.

Plaggen epipedon. A man-made surface horizon more than 50 cm thick with characteristics that depend upon the original soil from which it was derived.

Histic epipedon. A thin surface horizon, saturated with water for part of the year, and with a large amount of organic carbon.

Ochric epipedon. Epipedons which are too light in colour, too low in organic carbon, or too thin to belong to the above.

Sub-surface diagnostic horizons, of which there are thirteen, occur below these surface horizons. The following brief descriptions summarise the detailed explanations given:

Argillic horizon. An illuvial horizon in which clays have accumulated to a significant extent.

Agric horizon. A compact horizon formed by cultivation which has been enriched by clay and/or humus.

Natric horizon. An argillic horizon with columnar structure and more than 15 per cent saturated with exchangeable sodium ions.

Spodic horizon. A horizon with an accumulation of free sesquioxides and/or organic carbon but not with equivalent amounts of crystalline clay.

Cambic horizon. A changed or altered horizon, including structure formation, liberation of free iron oxides, clay formation or the obliteration of the original structure of the parent material.

Oxic horizon. A horizon with a very low content of weatherable minerals, in which the clay is composed of kaolinite and sesquioxides, having a low cation exchange capacity and poorly dispersable in water.

Calcic horizon. Enriched horizon with calcium carbonate in the form of secondary concentrations, more than 15 cm. thick.

Gypsic horizon. Enriched horizon with calcium sulphate, more than 15 cm. thick.

Salic horizon. Enriched horizon with salts more soluble than gypsum, more than 15 cm. thick.

Albic horizon. A horizon from which clay and free iron oxides have been removed, so the colour is determined by the colour of sand and silt and not the coatings on these particles.

Other horizons which are identified include the indurated horizons of certain soils. The *duripan* is a horizon cemented by silica or aluminium silicate. The *fragipan* is a loamy sub-surface horizon with platy structure and high bulk density, brittle when wet and hard when dry. A *petrocalcic* is a continuous, indurated horizon, cemented with calcium carbonate. *Plinthite* is rich in sesquioxides, highly weathered and poor in humus which irreversibly hardens into crusts and irregular aggregates when dried.

To place a soil in this classification it is necessary to use a key which can be found in the original monograph and its successive supplements. However, a recent American publication gives a simplified version which may be used in a semi-quantitative manner to allocate soils within the ten orders (Table 5.4).

Soils are formed from one or a number of horizons and in the system employed the smallest volume of soil recognisable is a *pedon*. This is defined as three-dimensional unit with a vague and arbitary lower limit but with lateral dimensions large enough to study the nature of the horizons present. Usually, this will involve an area of between 1 and 10 sq. m. A *polypedon* usually will contain two or more pedons and these form the *soil series*, of which there are estimated to be at least 10,000 in the United States alone. The series are related through *families* which stress common conditions for plant growth, *subgroups* to *great groups*. There are approximately 206 *great groups* in which the presence or absence of the diagnostic horizons becomes an important criterion. The great groups are arranged in 47 *suborders* characterised by similar genetic processes; subdivision is by presence or absence of wetness, soil moisture regime, climatic regimes and, in histosols, the stage of organic fibre decomposition. The sub-

Table 5.4 *Simplified key to soil orders, American soil survey staff classification*

If a soil has:	
30% clay to 1 m. or to rock or unaltered parent material with gilgai, slickensides or wedge-shaped aggregates	Vertisol
No diagnostic horizon other than ochric, anthropic, albic or agric	Entisol
No spodic, argillic, natric, oxic, petrocalcic plinthite but with cambic or histic horizon	Inceptisol
Ochric or argillic but no oxic or spodic horizon and usually dry	Aridisol
Spodic horizon	Spodosol
Mean annual temperature 8°C, properties not placing it in one of the above, percentage base saturation 35 at 1.25 m. below the top of an argillic horizon or 1.80 m. below the surface	Ultisol
Mollic but no oxic horizon	Mollisol
All other mineral horizons without oxic	Alfisols
Oxic horizon	Oxisol
30% organic matter to a depth of 40 cm.	Histosol
(After Buol, Hole and McCracken)	

orders are finally arranged in ten *orders* in which the soil forming processes are indicated by the presence of absence of the major diagnostic horizons described previously. The orders and suborders of the classification are given in Table 5.5.

Table 5.5 *American soil survey staff soil classification Soil Taxonomy (1975)*

1. Entisols. Weakly developed (generally azonal) soils	
— with features of gleying	Aquents
— with strong artificial disturbance	Arents
— on alluvial deposits	Fluvents
— with sand or loamy sand texture	Psamments
— other Entisols (e.g. lithosols, some regosols)	Orthents
2. Vertisols. Cracking clay soils	
— usually moist	Uderts
— dry for short periods	Usterts
— dry for a long period	Xererts
— usually dry	Torrerts

41

3. Inceptisols. Moderately developed soils, not in other orders
   - with features of gleying — Aquepts
   - on volcanic ash — Andepts
   - in a tropical climate — Tropepts
   - with an umbric epipedon — Umbrepts
   - other Inceptisols (e.g. most brown earths) — Ochrepts
   - with plaggen epipedon — Plaggepts

4. Aridisols. Semi-desert and desert soils
   - with an argillic horizon — Argids
   - with soils of dry areas (e.g. grey desert soils) — Orthids

5. Mollisols. Soils with high base status with a dark A horizon
   - with albic and argillic horizons — Albolls
   - with features of gleying — Aquolls
   - on highly calcareous parent materials — Rendolls
   - others in cold climates — Borolls
   - others in humid climates — Udolls
   - others in sub-humid climates — Ustolls
   - others in sub-arid climates — Xerolls

6. Spodosols. Soils with a spodic horizon (e.g. podzols)
   - with features of gleying — Aquods
   - with little humus in spodic horizon — Ferrods
   - with little iron in spodic horizon — Humods
   - with iron and humus — Orthods

7. Alfisols. Soils with an argillic horizon and moderate to high base content
   - with features of gleying — Aqualfs
   - others in cold climates — Boralfs
   - others in humid climates — Udalfs
   - others in sub-humid climates — Ustalfs
   - others in sub-arid climates — Xeralfs

8. Ultisols. Soils with an argillic horizon and low base content
   - with features of gleying — Aquults
   - with a humose A horizon — Humults
   - in humid climates — Udults
   - others in sub-humid climates — Ustults
   - others in sub-arid climates — Xerults

9. Oxisols. Soils with an oxic horizon or with plinthite near the surface
   - with features of gleying — Aquox
   - with a humose A horizon — Humox
   - others in humid climates — Orthox
   - others in drier climates — Ustox
   - usually dry in most years — Torrox

10. Histosols. Soils developed in organic materials
    - never saturated for more than a few days, 75 per cent fibric material — Folists
    - saturated for six months or more, 75 per cent fibric material little decomposed — Fibrists
    - saturated for six months or more, partly altered organic material — Hemists
    - saturated for six months or more, highly decomposed fibric content — Saprists

As can be seen from the above table, the name of the soil sub-orders are compounded from certain formative elements derived from the name of the soil order. Prefixes such as aqu-characters associated with wetness, ud-characters associated with humid climates and ust-characters associated with dry climates, are added to suggest the properties of the sub-order. Further adjectival prefixes give rise to the great group names. Although the introduction of the American system has stimulated much discussion and many references have been made to it, it has not been adopted in Britain or Europe by the soil survey organisations, but is increasingly used as an international standard of comparison for soils.

It is unfortunate that many soil classifications have been based upon the presence or absence of certain types of soil humus, for this can easily be changed by clearance or cultivation. Transient features are not the best ones for criteria in a classification. It has already been seen that texture forms a good basis for classification, being one of the more stable features of the soil. Other of the more persistent features are the nature and quantity of the clay minerals present, the amount and type of the exchangeable cations, and the degree of leaching. All of these have been incorporated into a scheme of classification proposed by Hallsworth which seems to have much to offer in a pedological approach to world soils (Table 5.6).

Table 5.6 *Classification of soils by extent of leaching (After Hallsworth, 1965)*

0. Soils showing no or only rudimentary differentiation
   e.g. Lithosols, Alluvial soils

1. Soils effectively unleached containing soluble salts, mainly sodium chloride e.g. Solonchak

2. Slightly leached soils (2nd stage of leaching) dominated by sodium ions, often containing gypsum e.g. Solonetz, Sierozems.

3. Moderately leached soils (3rd stage of leaching) dominated by Ca (Mg) ions and containing secondary carbonate
   e.g. Chernozems, Chestnut soils

4. Moderately leached soils (4th stage of leaching) dominated by Ca (H) ions and without secondary carbonate
   e.g. Brown soils, Argillic brown soils

5. Strongly leached soils (5th stage of leaching) dominated by H, Al (Fe) ions
   e.g. Podzols, Ferrallitic soils

At the instigation of the International Society of Soil Science, a soil map of the world is currently being produced by a joint panel of soil scientists from F.A.O. and U.N.E.S.C.O. At the time of writing (1976) the maps of North and South America as well as Africa and Southern Asia are available. The legend for this new world map contains soil units which have been distinguished on the basis of the present knowledge of their genesis, morphology and distribution as well as upon their significance as a natural resource for food production. Following the trend established by the American system, diagnostic horizons have been used to distinguish different soil groupings. Where possible, traditional names have been retained but where doubt or confusion surrounded the use of an older term, it has been omitted and a new name selected. The brief descriptions which follow (Table 5.7) are not definitions, but are given to introduce the reader to the terminology of the soil mapping units shown on this important new map.

In Chapters 6 to 10 the appropriate classification of soils is given in brackets following the name in conventional or colloquial use. The U.S. Soil Taxonomy name is given first and the F.A.O./U.N.E.S.C.O. Legend name second following a semicolon. e.g. (Dystrochrept; Cambisol).

Table 5.7 *Brief definitions of soil units from F.A.O./U.N.E.S.C.O. Soil map of the world*

Fluvisols (from Latin fluvius, river; connotative of floodplains and alluvial deposits). Weakly developed soils from alluvial deposits in active floodplains

Regosols (from Greek rhegos, blanket; connotative of mantle of loose material)

Arenosols (from Latin arena, sand). Strongly weathered sandy soils of tropical and subtropical areas

Gleysols (from Russian local name 'gley' meaning mucky soil mass; connotative of reduced or mottled layers resulting from an excess of water). Soils in which the hydromorphic processes are dominant

Rendzinas (from Polish rzedzic, noise; connotative of plough noise in shallow soils). Soils developed surface horizons rich in organic matter over highly calcareous materials

Rankers (from Austrian rank, steep slope; connotative of shallow soils). Soils which develop a surface horizon enriched in organic matter over siliceous materials

Andosols (from Japanese an, dark and do, soil; connotative of soils formed from materials rich in volcanic glass and commonly having a dark surface horizon). Weakly developed soils, rich in allophane and having a low bulk density

Vertisols (from Latin verto, turn; connotative of a turn over of surface soil, self-mulching soils). Black, cracking clay soils

Yermosols (from Spanish yermo, desert, derived from Latin eremus, solitary, desolate). Soils of desert environments

Xerosols (from Greek xeros, dry). Soils of semi-arid environments

Solonchaks (from Russian sol, salt). Soils showing strong salinity

Solonetz (from Russian sol, salt). Soils developed under the influence of high sodium saturation

Planosols (from Latin planus, flat, level); connotative of soils generally developed in level or depressed topography with poor drainage

Greyzems (from grey and Russian zemlja, earth, land). Soils of the forest-steppe transition, rich in organic matter and having a grey colour caused by white silica powder on structure faces

Kastanozems (from Latin castaneo, chestnut, and from Russian zemlja, earth, land). Soils of the semi-arid steppes showing an accumulation of organic matter in the surface horizons, often calcareous throughout

Chernozems (from Russian chern, black and zemlja, earth, land). Soils of the grassland steppes showing strong accumulation of organic matter in the surface horizons and an accumulation of calcium carbonate at shallow depth.

Phaeozems (from Greek phaios, dusky, and Russian zemlja, earth, land). Soils of the forest-steppes showing a strong accumulation of organic matter in the surface but a deep leaching of calcium carbonate

Cambisols (from Latin cambiare, change; connotative of soils in which changes in colour, structure, and consistence have taken place as a result of weathering). Soils formed by a weak alteration of the parent material

Luvisols (from Latin luvi, from luo, to wash, lessiver; connotative of illuvial accumulation of clay). Soils having an argillic B horizon of medium to high base status

Acrisols (from Latin acris, very acid). Soils having an argillic B horizon and of low base saturation

Podzols (from Russian local name derived from pod, under and zola, ash). Soils with a strongly bleached horizon having B horizons with iron or humus accumulation, or both

Podzoluvisols (combined Podzol and Luvisol). Soils having an argillic B horizon but also showing features of Podzols

Nitosols (from Latin nitidus, shiny, bright, lustrous; connotative of shiny ped faces). Soils having very deeply developed argillic B horizons and showing features of strong weathering

Ferralsols (from Latin ferrum and aluminium; connotative of a high content of sesquioxides). Strongly weathered soils consisting mainly of kaolinite, quartz and hydrated oxides

Histosols (from Greek histos, tissue). Organic soils

Lithosols (from Greek lithos, stone). Shallow soils over hard rock

The Soil Survey of England and Wales adopted a new classification in 1973 (Table 5.8). In a similar manner to the American and the World Map systems of classification, this British system has a limited number of diagnostic horizons. These include podzolic B horizons (containing enrichment with organic matter, amorphous iron and aluminium), argillic B horizons (with pedological re-organisation but not enrichment) and gleyed B horizons (showing reduction and segregation or loss of iron), as well as different forms of surface horizons. This classification has evolved from previous work and retains many names currently familiar to users of soil maps. Several new features are included which aim to give a more satisfactory grouping of British soils and to maintain a working relationship with classifications developed in the Netherlands, France and Germany as

Table 5.8 *Classification of soils in England and Wales (Avery, 1973).*

Major Group	Group
1. Terrestrial raw soils	1.1 Raw sands
	1.2 Raw alluvial soils
	1.3 Raw skeletal soils
	1.4 Raw earths
	1.5 Man-made raw soils
2. Hydric raw soils	2.1 Raw sandy gley soils
	2.2 Un-ripened gley soils
3. Lithomorphic soils	3.1 Rankers
	3.2 Sand-rankers
	3.3 Ranker-like alluvial soils
	3.4 Rendzinas
	3.5 Pararendzinas
	3.6 Sand pararendzinas
	3.7 Rendzina-like alluvial soils

4. Pelosols	4.1 Calcareous pelosols
	4.2 Non-calcareous pelosols
	4.3 Argillic pelosols
5. Brown soils	5.1 Brown calcareous earths
	5.2 Brown calcareous sands
	5.3 Brown calcareous alluvial soils
	5.4 Brown earths
	5.5 Brown sands
	5.6 Brown alluvial soils
	5.7 Argillic brown earths
	5.8 Paleo-argillic brown earths
6. Podzolic soils	6.1 Brown podzolic soils
	6.2 Humic cryptopodzols
	6.3 Podzols
	6.4 Gley podzols
	6.5 Stagno podzols
7. Surface-water gley (Stagnogley soils)	7.1 Stagnogley soils
	7.2 Stagno humic gley soils
8. Ground-water gley-soils	8.1 Alluvial gley soils
	8.2 Sandy gley soils
	8.3 Cambic gley soils
	8.4 Argillic gley soils
	8.5 Humic alluvial gley soils
	8.6 Humic sandy gley soils
	8.7 Humic gley soils
9. Man-made soils	9.1 Man-made humus soils
	9.2 Disturbed soils
10. Peat (Organic) soils	10.1 Raw peat soils
	10.2 Earthy peat soils

well as with the American and World Soil Map systems.

Of the ten major groups in this classification, some are recognisable immediately whilst others are new or re-organised. Major departures from previous classifications include the Litho-morphic soils which bring together AC soils such as rendzinas and rankers. Pelosols are a small group of clayey soils typically found on calcareous argillaceous materials which possess vertic properties, i.e. they expand and contract markedly with wetting and drying. The brown soils and the podzols have undergone stricter definition but the controversial brown podzolic

group, with podzolic B horizons and lacking bleached eluvial horizons, has been allocated to the podzol group. Stricter definition is apparent also in the two major groups of poorly drained soils, now brought more closely into line with the European concepts of pseudogley and gley. The difference here is either the retention of water within the profiles – stagnogley conditions, or the presence of a fluctuating, high water-table. The presence of man-made soils as a major group reflects historical influences of man in enriching the surface horizons of plaggen soils. Throughout the whole system the texture is an important criterion with separation of clayey soils as pelosols at major group level and loamy from sandy soils at group level. At subgroup level the classification distinguishes typical soils as well as other variations denoted by the adjectival use of the words humic, cambic, vertic, ferric, argillic and gleyic should the diagnostic horizon meet with the necessary criteria. There are over 100 of these subgroups proposed, so it is impossible to discuss each individually.

It is the intention to present in this book a review of the main soil types of the world in a geographical or environmental framework. Because of the complexity at local level a consideration of soils on a world basis has many disadvantages and inevitably vague generalisations are made. However it is important to realise that many correlations can be drawn between the different factors of the environment which together produce the soil cover. In fact the soil can be considered to be the product of all these factors or, in other words, to form a zonal index which signifies a degree of environmental uniformity in the area covered by a particular soil type. The placing of soils in the different latitudinal zones is following the tradition of Russian soil scientists who, with their opportunity to study soils over continental areas, have one of the best overall views of world soils. As the climate is of fundamental importance, the following discussion of the soils of the world is based on a broad climatic/latitudinal scheme (Table 5.9).

As these zones cover large areas and diverse climates mention is made of the climatic conditions where the typical soils are found. Because vegetation responds to the influence of climate

Table 5.9 *A simplified zonal classification of soils*

Latitude zone	Bio-climatic zone	Zonal soils (common names)
1. Soils of the high latitudes	Tundra	Arctic brown soils Arctic gley soils
2. Soils of the mid-latitudes, cool climates	Northern coniferous forests and heaths	Podzols Brown podzolic soils
	Deciduous woodlands	Brown soils Argillic brown soils
	Wooded steppes	Grey soils
3. Soils of the mid-latitudes, warm climates	Mixed moist evergreen woodlands	Brown Mediterranean soils Red Mediterranean soils
	Mixed dry evergreen woodlands	Cinnamon soils
	Mixed oak, pine with summer rainfall	Red podzolic soils Yellow podzolic soils
	Steppe grasslands	Chernozems
	Dry steppe grasslands	Chestnut soils
	Semi-desert	Sierozems
	Desert	Raw mineral soils
4. Soils of the low latitudes	Tropical rain forest and deciduous forests	Ferrallitic soils Podzols
	Tropical grasslands	Ferruginous soils Vertisols Laterite
	Man-modified soils	Acid sulphate soils Paddy soils

and soil, at world level of mapping there is a fairly close correlation between the occurrence of world plant formations and world soils. However, the world plant formation distribution maps, as in the case of soil maps, mask a great variation at local level where parent material and differing hydrological conditions can modify the vegetation and soil type. The presentation here of the associated *intrazonal* and *azonal* soils representative of the different bio-climatic zones is an attempt to overcome the disadvantage of suggesting any one soil for any one bio-climatic zone. The soil properties and distribution will be discussed in the text and the illustrations show relations to landforms in idealised landscapes.

Intrazonal soils
Calcimorphic soils
Hydromorphic soils
Halomorphic soils
Andosols

Azonal soils
Lithosols
Regosols
Alluvial soils
Mountain soils
Organic soils

From this chapter it is evident that there are many different ways of classifying soils, and that each system has its merits. However, amongst soil scientists classification is one of the most hotly debated subjects. As Leeper puts it in a discussion of soil classification 'when scientists discuss methods of analysing a solution for traces of phosphate they are practical, reasonable and unemotional. When the same men discuss the classification of soils these virtues are likely to evaporate'. The problems of soil classification are bound up with local and national prestige, for decisions taken at a local level often cannot be accommodated at a national or international level.

6 SOILS OF THE HIGH LATITUDES

The largest areas of tundra soils are found in the northern hemisphere surrounding the Arctic Ocean. The distribution of these soils in Eurasia extends northwards of a line from the extreme north of Norway, across the north of Siberia approximately along the line of the Arctic Circle, reaching the coast again in the region of the Kamchatka Peninsula (Fig. 6.1). A similar distribution is seen in North America where the line extends along the arctic coast of Alaska, to the Great Bear Lake, the southwestern shore of Hudson Bay, crossing the Labrador – Ungava Peninsula to reach the Atlantic coast. Altogether approximately 4 per cent of the land area of the world has tundra soils.

The tundra is characterised by a severe climate with long, bitterly cold winters and short cool summers. Tundra climate (ET) as defined by Köppen has two to four months only of average temperatures above freezing, and a killing frost

6.1 Distribution of permafrost in the tundra regions of the northern hemisphere

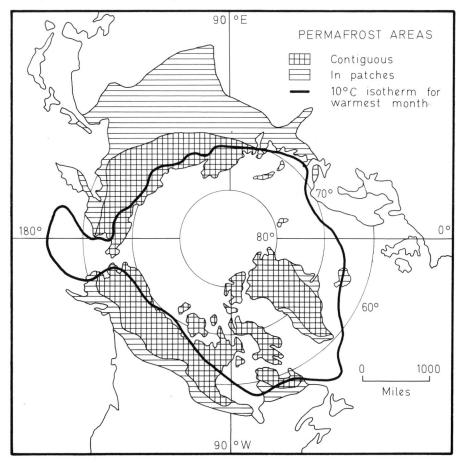

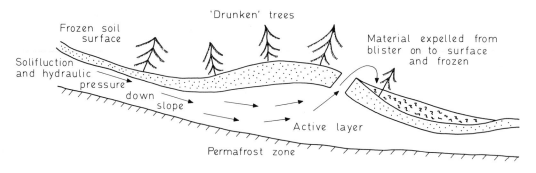

6.2 A soil blister or pingo; water from the slope descends under hydraulic pressure and lifts the frozen surface soil in a blister up to 7 metres high

can occur at any time. Winter temperatures are as low as $-35°C$ or $-40°C$. Tundra regions also have a low precipitation, usually 250 to 300 mm. per annum.

In the southern hemisphere tundra soils are less extensive, but they do occur on areas of Antarctica not covered by ice, the elevated areas of the Andes, the Great Dividing Range in the southeast of Australia, and in the Southern Alps of New Zealand. Tundra soils can be seen at high altitude on mountains in other parts of the world, but their extent is strictly limited to the higher peaks of mountains.

The parent materials of soils in the tundra are diverse, ranging in age from Pre-Cambrian shield areas of Canada and Siberia to the Cretaceous of Spitzbergen and the boulder clay and alluvium of more recent time. The local rocks will be slowly weathered by physical processes chiefly, and weathering will tend to be concentrated in the periods when an alternation of freezing and thawing takes place.

Below the soil in the tundra regions is a layer of permanently frozen ground, known as the *permafrost*. It represents the soil and rock which is not thawed out during the brief period of the arctic or antarctic summer. The soil which does become thawed during the summer is saturated with water which cannot escape downwards by percolation because of the permafrost layer beneath. In these conditions the soil becomes so wet that it can flow gently downslope, a process which is called *solifluction*. As a result of pressures generated when the surface horizons freeze, the still liquid material lying above the permafrost sometimes erupts on the surface forming

mounds known as *pingos* (Fig. 6.2). Thus there is a continuing process of redistribution of soil matter associated with each period of freeze and thaw. The general result is for the material to move downslope and at the same time to become roughly sorted with the finer material occupying the lower parts of the landscape leaving thin soils with coarse rock fragments on the hills.

The 'cold deserts' are those parts of the world in polar regions and amongst high mountains which are not currently covered by glacier ice. They are treeless with the tree line marking their boundaries. This is approximately shown by the 10 °C isotherm for the warmest month (Fig. 6.1). In the tundra, the depth of rooting for trees is limited by the permafrost, and although water is plentiful during period of thaw, for much of the year it is unavailable because it is frozen. Growing vegetation can therefore experience a physiological drought, which is estimated as a deficiency of up to 170 mm. at Barrow, Alaska, an environment which can be classed as semi-arid. At the boundary of the tundra, where sheltered sites permit, spruce, larch, pine, birch, aspen, willow and mountain ash will grow. However, their growth is slow, and they are frequently small and deformed because of the severe climate. On the tundra itself, heather, arctic blueberry, as well as flowering plants such as buttercups and mountain avens, lichens and mosses are the most common where other plants cannot survive.

Although the rate of plant growth is slow, so is the rate of decomposition of organic matter, consequently there is a slow accumulation of organic matter in these soils. Soil formation is essentially restricted to the summer when the upper layers of the soil thaw. Precipitation is slight, either as rain or snow, so that even at the low temperature then experienced evaporation can exceed precipitation. In all probability the water which leaches these soils comes from the melting snow in early summer. Where the permafrost is close to the surface downward leaching is clearly limited, and only where it is deeper in the soil and the soil is permeable can normal horizon differentiation take place. Obviously this will be on the margin of the tundra zone and in favourable sites only.

Any tendency towards horizon development is countered by the process of churning which occurs in the 'active' layer. Because the soil freezes from the surface downwards, a saturated layer of soil is trapped between it and the permafrost. As there is expansion in the process of freezing, pressures are built up which eventually rupture the surface, spilling the lower material on to it. This churning process is referred to as *cryoturbation*. This process, with the solifluction mentioned previously, inhibits the development of horizons which are the characteristic features of the soils of temperate climates.

The sorting processes produce a soil catena which has been described from Spitsbergen by Smith (Fig. 6.3). Upper slopes are characterised by frost shattering, and screes at angles of 34° develop below the outcrop of solid rocks. The movement downslope of loose materials merges into a striped pattern of gravel with finer soils between (Plate 1). The stripes occur on slopes up to 25°. Lower-angled slopes of 12–4° are characterised by soils showing signs of solifluction with irregularly shaped terraces of bare mud. Slopes of less than 4° develop polygonal soils with elevated mud centres. The lowest parts of the landscape are covered with peat deposits.

Arctic brown soils

If a case is to be made for a mature soil which could be said to be characteristic of the tundra, the arctic brown soils (Cryochrepts; Gelic Cambisols)* described from Alaska would seem to have the necessary qualifications. This soil occurs on ridge tops, escarpment edges, terrace edges and other places where free drainage occurs. The soil is dark brown in colour and has fragile fine-crumb structure in the A horizon. A dark yellow-brown B horizon of sandy loam overlies a horizon of shattered sandstone bedrock.

Profile of an arctic brown soil (Cryochrept; Gelic Cambisol) from Alaska
(Parent material – sandstone)

2– 0 cm.	Black organic layer
0–17 cm.	Dark brown (7.5YR3/2) sandy loam with single grain to fine crumb structure. Very loose and friable.
17–36 cm.	Dark yellow-brown (10YR3/4) sandy loam with single grain to fine crumb structure. Loose and friable
36–60 cm.	Dark yellow-brown (10YR4/4) sandy loam. Firm but friable
60–80 cm.	Very dark grey-brown (2.5YR3/2). Loamy sand with small weakly indurated aggregates. Numerous small rock fragments
80 cm. +	Shattered bedrock with numerous sandstone fragments

(After Tedrow)

Note. Symbols following colour descriptions refer to the notation used in the Munsell Soil Colour Charts (p. 107).

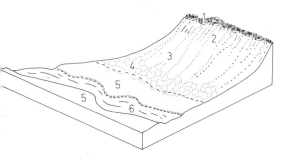

6.3 A block diagram illustrating relationships of soils found in tundra regions
1. Frost-shattered rock on ridge crests.
2. Scree on steep slopes over 25°.
3. Stone stripes on slopes 12°–24°.
4. Arctic gley soils on fine solifluction material (polygon soils).
5. Arctic brown soils on river terrace materials.
6. Alluvial material in valley bottoms

*U.S. Soil Taxonomy name and F.A.O./U.N.E.S.C.O. name respectively see p. 43.

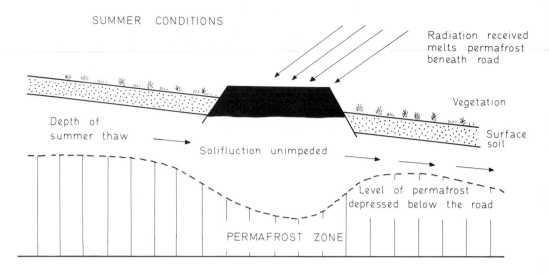

SUMMER CONDITIONS

Radiation received melts permafrost beneath road

Vegetation

Surface soil

Depth of summer thaw

Solifluction unimpeded

Level of permafrost depressed below the road

PERMAFROST ZONE

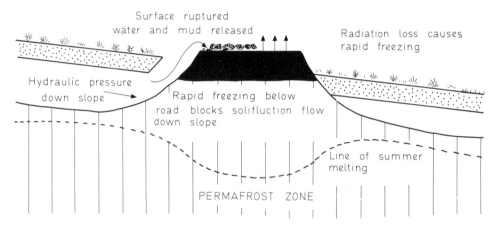

EARLY WINTER

Surface ruptured water and mud released

Radiation loss causes rapid freezing

Hydraulic pressure down slope

Rapid freezing below road blocks solifluction flow down slope

Line of summer melting

PERMAFROST ZONE

6.4 The effect of a road upon soil in the tundra

Arctic gley soils

The area of freely drained soils is limited. More typical of the tundra is a gley or peaty gley soil formed with conditions of poor drainage. On clay-rich parent materials, a Russian author has described an arctic gley soil (Cryaquents; Gelic Gleysols) from Wrangel Island where above the permafrost a gley horizon of 44 cm. underlies this organic-rich (5 per cent) A horizon. The formative element cry- indicates a soil has a temperature regime of less than 8°C in the American system and the word gelic implies the presence of permanently frozen ground within 200 cm. of the soil surface for the World Soil Map Legend.

Profile of an arctic gley soil (Cryaquent; Geli Gleysol) from Wrangel Island
(Parent material — river terrace deposit)

2– 0 cm. Peaty, part-decomposed plant remain

0– 1 cm. Brown clay loam with fine (crumb? structure and roots

1–44 cm. Grey light-blue with yellow horizonta streaks of clay loam with fine structures, porous, some plant root extending to 38 cm

44 cm +. Permafrost

(After Svatkov

50

The relationships of the arctic gley soil and the arctic brown soils are shown in Fig. 6.3. Other soils which have been described from arctic tundra regions are transitional to the podzols, gley podzols and peat. Salt-enriched solonchak soils also occur where salts accumulate at the foot of slopes or where salt spray is driven inland and accumulates in the soils. Thus in spite of the severity of the climate and limitation on soil-forming processes there is considerable range of soils to be seen in tundra regions. Tundra soils are variously allocated in the U.S. Soil Taxonomy to cryic great groups of the orders such as the Entisols, Inceptisols, and Spodosols, e.g. Cryaquents – polygonal soils; Cryaquods – ground-water podzols. The F.A.O./U.N.E.S.C.O. World Soil Map indicates large areas of Gelic Regosols and Gelic Gleysols in northern Canada, bordering Hudson Bay and the Arctic Ocean. Lithosols are extensive in the northern Ungava peninsula.

Interest in tundra soils has been stimulated by strategic needs during the last three decades in both Russia and North America. Also the extraction of valuable minerals and oil from the arctic regions necessitated the building and maintenance of pipelines, road and rail communications. The engineering problems encountered led to considerable research which has revealed additional information about the area and its soils (Fig. 6.4). Houses built directly on the soil surface melt the permafrost and warm oil-pipelines can initiate irreparable damage by erosion when normally frozen soils are thawed.

The importance of the study of tundra soils lies in the fact that during the Pleistocene their extent was much greater and included much of North America, Europe and the British Isles where relic features of tundra soils are widespread. Features variously known as involutions, convolutions or festoons which can be attributed to the churning movements of the former active layer can be seen in sections revealed in quarries (Fig. 6.5). The upper layer of the permafrost became compacted by ice growth and infilling by silt to form an undurated horizon which has been described from many soils in Scotland and Wales. Wedges of ice which penetrated deeply into the weathered mantle during the last cold period eventually melted out and the space left became

6.5 The effect of a periglacial climate can be seen in features known as involutions or festoons

6.6 An ice wedge pseudomorph. This feature once occupied by ice has been filled by different material A which distinguished it from the surrounding chalk B

infilled with material of a different nature. These infillings, fossil ice wedges, can also be seen in quarry sections of gravel, sand or chalky material (Fig. 6.6). An example of polygonal ground formed during a previous cold period is exposed on the Cardigan Bay, where it was covered by a later deposit which the sea is eroding once again (Fig. 6.7). Fossil pingoes have been found in central Wales and East Anglia, having a raised rim and a collapsed core, now occupied by an accumulation of peat (Fig. 6.8).

An understanding of tundra soils is necessary to interpret the features seen in the subsoils of many American, British and European soils, the distribution of whose parent materials is impossible to explain without reference to periglacial climate. As the surface horizons may have been changed by the current soil-forming factors so the soils are appropriate for the area, but below is concealed the evidence of an earlier period of different climate and soil-forming processes.

6.7 Frost polygons. Constant freeze-thaw activity results in sorting coarse from fine material. The coarse material is pushed into a polygonal pattern

6.8 A fossil pingo. The ice core has melted and the centre has collapsed leaving a circular mound filled with peat

7 SOILS OF THE MID-LATITUDES, COOL CLIMATES

Four 'zonal' soils can be considered as typical of the cool temperate climates; podzols, brown soils, argillic brown soils and grey soils. Although there is considerable climatic variation in the mid-latitude areas of cool climate, there is sufficient precipitation to maintain an overall downward leaching of any soluble soil constituents. The podsol is typical of more northern areas where it is associated with the boreal forests; however, podzols can also be seen where heath plants occupy infertile sandy or gravelly areas within the deciduous forest areas. Brown earths and grey-brown podzolic soils are normally associated with the deciduous forest, and the grey soils with the forest-steppe transition. Synonyms of these soils in common use in the U.S. Soil Taxonomy and the F.A.O./U.N.E.S.C.O. World Map Legend are given in Table 7.1.

Within this broad zone of soil formation, there are many divergences from the zonal types. These divergences occur because of the interplay of parent material, vegetation, accumulation of organic matter, soil drainage or stage of maturity. Thus, within this zone, intrazonal rendzinas, rankers, gley and organic soils can be identified in addition to the azonal skeletal soils (Orthents, Lithosols) and those formed from recent alluvium (Fluvents; Fluvisols). These soils have in common the fact that they are all leached to some extent. The different zonal soils groups are differentiated by the visual appearance of their profiles, though sub-groups may need some laboratory investigation for their accurate identification.

Podzols
These soils are characterised by the presence, just below the surface, of an ashy-coloured horizon

Table 7.1 *Synonyms for soils in the mid-latitudes, cool climates*

Common Names	U.S. Soil Taxonomy	F.A.O./U.N.E.S.C.O. World Map Legend
Podzols		
Podzols (humus iron)	Orthods	Orthic podzols
Iron podzols	Ferrods	Ferric podzols
Humus podzols	Humods	Humic Podzols
Brown podzolic soils	Haplorthods	Leptic podzols
Brown soils		
Brown earths	Eutrochrepts	Eutric cambisols
Acid brown earths	Dystrochrepts	Dystric cambisols
Argillic brown soils		
Grey brown podzolic soils	Hapludalfs	Orthic luvisols
Sols lessivés		
Grey soils		
Derno-podzolic soils	Glossudalfs Glossoboralfs	Eutric podzoluvisols
Grey wooded soils	Eutroboralfs Cryoboralfs	Albic luvisols
Grey forest soils	Argiborolls	Orthic greyzems

from which they derive their Russian peasant name. On world soil maps podzols are shown as extending in a circumpolar belt approximately from the Arctic Circle southwards to 50° N in Eurasia, and slightly further south, to the latitude of the Great Lakes in North America (Fig. 11.1). South of this main circumpolar zone, podzols are restricted to areas where a combination of parent material, climate and vegetation are favourable for their development. Podzols are found also in limited areas of Australia and South America, and where higher mountains or suitable parent materials occur. (A form of podzol can also be seen in the tropics where deep profiles have developed on alluvial sands, p. 86.) Within the main podzol zone in the northern hemisphere, large areas of the earth's surface are mantled with Pleistocene fluvio-glacial deposits. Although podzolization proceeds most rapidly upon permeable sands and gravels, soils of this type can be found on a wide range of different parent materials including sandstones, siltstones, clays and in certain circumstances even soils partly derived from limestones.

The climates associated with the development of podzol soils have cold winters and short, warm summers. In European Russia, these soils are frozen for at least five months of the year, and during the brief summer temperatures only reach between 15 °C and 19 °C. In this typically continental climate, winter precipitation is in the form of snow, and about half the annual precipitation is in the form of summer rain. The total amount of precipitation is not great, 500–550 mm. are stated as average for Eurasia, but amounts of up to 1000 mm. occur in North America. In terms of Thornthwaite's evapotranspiration figures, the main podzol zone lies between the 400–500 mm. lines, and according to Köppen the southern boundary is approximately that of the 'cold zone' which experiences a temperature of over 10 °C in the warmest month and below −33 °C in the coldest month. Podzols are found predominantly in Köppen's humid microthermal climates (Dfa, Dfb, Dwa, Dwb) as well as in sub-arctic climates (Dfc, Dwc, Dwd) and marine west coast climates (Cfb). The freezing conditions of winter months in the colder areas largely inhibit the soil-forming tendencies, but with the snow-melt of spring,

considerable moisture is available, and leaching and gleying of the soil profile occur.

Podzols (Orthods; Orthic, Ferric and Humic Podzols) are soils associated with heath and the coniferous forests of northern latitudes, alternatively known as the boreal forest or taiga. In Europe this forest is composed of spruce, pine, larch and birch; in Siberia, the Dahurian larch is dominant in the areas of the most extreme climatic ranges; and in the Far East, fir becomes co-dominant with spruce. The number of species in the American boreal forests is greater, with spruce and fir growing on the better drained soils and black spruce and tamarack on the poorly drained soils. Burnt areas are colonised with jack pine, birch and aspen, while western forests are characterised by lodgepole pine and alpine fir. As the ecotone with the tundra is approached, the boreal forest thins and a discontinuous ground flora of crowberry and bilberry occurs as well as lichens such as *Cladonia*. South of the main podzol zone podzols may form beneath a mor humus derived from heath plants which have colonised acid sandy soils, this organic matter is noticeably deficient in bases and plant nutrients which are being returned to the soil. The acidity and the lack of light penetration to the forest floor reduce the number and range of organisms which should cause breakdown of plant material and humification. Breakdown of plant material is slow, mainly being achieved by the activity of fungi, with fauna such as mites being of secondary importance. The humus form is that of mor, in which the litter, fermentation and humus horizons can usually be identified. As earthworms are absent, incorporation into the soil is slow and thus a mat of organic material is gradually accumulated on the surface of the mineral soil.

A podzol soil is one in which a redistribution of the soil constituents has taken place by the downward-percolating rainwater. This water contains decomposition products from the vegetation and the organic matter described above. As it passes through the soil it can dissolve or extract any further soluble constituents. It has been shown that in acid conditions, such as are found in a podzol, fine particles of organic matter are capable of forming organo-mineral complexes which are carried down the profile. Several different explanations of the way in which iron can be moved from the A and Ea horizons have been put forward including chemical, physical and biological processes. However, although much work has been done on this problem, there is as yet no unanimous agreement about what is involved. It is certain that constituents are removed and redeposited lower in the soil profile. Because of the removal of constituents, notably iron and aluminium, and the breakdown of clays, there is a relative increase in the amount of silica remaining in the Ea horizon and an increase in the amount of sesquioxides or iron and aluminium in the Bs horizon. This process results in the distinctive horizons of the podzol profile (Fig. 7.1).

In modern systems of soil classification, soils can belong to the podzols (Spodosols) only if they possess a B horizon with certain defined characteristics. In the U.S. Soil Taxonomy the diagnostic horizon required is the *spodic horizon*. This should be at least 1 cm. thick and contain substantial amounts of carbon, iron and aluminium (extractable by potassium pyrophosphate solution) in relation to the amount of clay with certain micromorphological characteristics and hues of 10 YR or redder. Similar requirements are necessary for inclusion in the podzols of the F.A.O./U.N.E.S.C.O. legend and in many national soil classifications. As an example the British podzolic B horizon must contain more than 0.3 per cent extractable iron and aluminium amount-

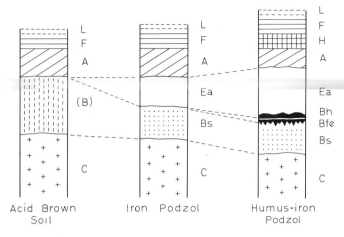

7.2 Maturity sequence of soils from acid brown soil to humus-iron podzol (after Mackney)

ing to at least 5 per cent of the clay percentage. It is interesting to note in passing that the emphasis has changed from the original Russian bleached eluvial horizon to the illuvial horizons of the profile and that the name podzolic, in the case of the Soil Survey of England and Wales, has been applied now to the B and not the E horizon.

There are a number of variations which may be seen in the field examinations of these soils. On lowland sites it has been suggested that some of these variations may be linked in a maturity sequence. This begins with a podzolic acid brown soil or brown podzolic soil with weakly developed Ea and Bs horizons, continues with an iron podzol in which the oxides of iron have been moved to form the Bs horizon, and culminates in the most mature soil, the humus-iron podzol (Fig. 7.2 and Plate 2). In this soil an accumulation of organic material, a Bh horizon, occurs in and above the Bfe and Bs horizons, suggesting that the organic matter is arrested in its progress down the profile by the increasing accumulation of iron. This stage is associated with a heathland vegetation in northwestern Europe. Parent materials lacking in iron cannot develop a humus-iron podzol profile, and certain dune sand deposits in Holland have well formed humus podzols (Humods; Humic Podzols) in which the Bfe and Bs horizons are absent (Plate 3). Horizon sequences are given in Table 7.2.

7.1 Diagrammatic profile of a humus-iron podzol

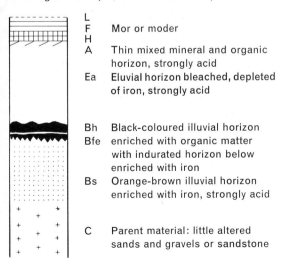

	L	
	F	Mor or moder
	H	
	A	Thin mixed mineral and organic horizon, strongly acid
	Ea	Eluvial horizon bleached, depleted of iron, strongly acid
	Bh	Black-coloured illuvial horizon
	Bfe	enriched with organic matter with indurated horizon below enriched with iron
	Bs	Orange-brown illuvial horizon enriched with iron, strongly acid
	C	Parent material: little altered sands and gravels or sandstone

Profile of a humus-iron podzol (Orthod; Orthic Podzol), *Derbyshire, England*
(Parent material – Bunter Pebble Beds)

L		Discontinuous litter of beech, oak and larch leaves
F	4–2.5 cm.	Comminuted, darkened and partly decomposed leaves
H	2.5–0 cm.	Black amorphous organic matter with a scatter of bleached sand grains
A	0–13 cm.	Very dark grey (10YR3/1) structureless sand with bleached grains; slightly stony with moderately high organic matter content; merging boundary
Ea	13–30 cm.	Grey (10YR5/1) structureless, slightly stony sand with bleached grains and low organic matter content; abrupt boundary.
Bh	30–31 cm.	Black (10YR2/1) indurated sand and stones with illuvial humus and iron accumulation; abrupt boundary
Bfe	31–32 cm.	Dark brown (7.5YR3/2) indurated sand and stones with illuvial iron accumulation; narrow boundary
Bs	32–40 cm.	Reddish-yellow to strong brown (7.5YR6/6 to 5/6) very stony compact sand with no apparent organic matter
C	40 cm. +	Bunter Pebble Beds

(After Bridges)

7.3 Diagrammatic profile of a ground-water podzol

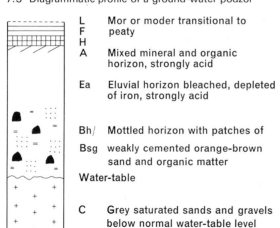

L		Mor or moder transitional to peaty
F		
H		
A		Mixed mineral and organic horizon, strongly acid
Ea		Eluvial horizon bleached, depleted of iron, strongly acid
Bh/		Mottled horizon with patches of
Bsg		weakly cemented orange-brown sand and organic matter
Water-table		
C		Grey saturated sands and gravels below normal water-table level

Where a high ground-water occurs in a pervious parent material undergoing podzolization, the normal processes are modified. A ground-water podzol forms which can have B horizons enriched with iron or organic matter or both (Aquods; Gleyic Podzols). The oxidation and reduction caused by alternate aerobic and anaerobic conditions gives the B horizon a mottled appearance with patches of weakly cemented orange-brown sand (Fig. 7.3 and Plate 4). In the podzol zone where wet conditions coincide with impervious parent materials gley or peaty gley soils usually result on lowland sites (Fig. 7.4). It should be noted that the Russian podzol includes many soils which the western pedologists would classify as hydromorphic soils, hence the great extent of podzol soils in northern Russia. In western Europe the podzol is thought of as a freely drained soil which occurs predominantly on lowland heaths.

Strong leaching and podzolization also occur on the uplands of western Europe where a form of podzol can be seen to have developed in a high rainfall regime. In an environment which has greater cloudiness, and a decreased rate of evapotranspiration, accumulation of an acid organic mat is encouraged. Gleying results below the mat and an Eag horizon develops. A thin iron pan, or placic horizon, which resembles a walnut shell in appearance, occurs below the Eag horizon. Water accumulating upon this pan adds to the gleying effect of the saturated superficial horizons (Fig. 7.5 and Plate 5). Below the iron pan, and in striking contrast, the soil is freely drained. This profile, which resembles the lowland podzol, is called a peaty gleyed podzol, and it is usually associated with peaty gleys and peats. In western Britain peaty gleyed podzols (Placaquods; Placic Podzols) frequently occur on the imperfectly drained sites on the upper convexity of hills (Fig. 7.6).

Profile of a peaty gleyed podzol (Placaquod; Placic Podzol), Shropshire, England
(Parent Material – hard Longmyndian shales)

F	10–7.5 cm.	Partly decomposed plant remains
H	7.5–0 cm.	Black amorphous organic matter with pieces of charcoal and many heather roots

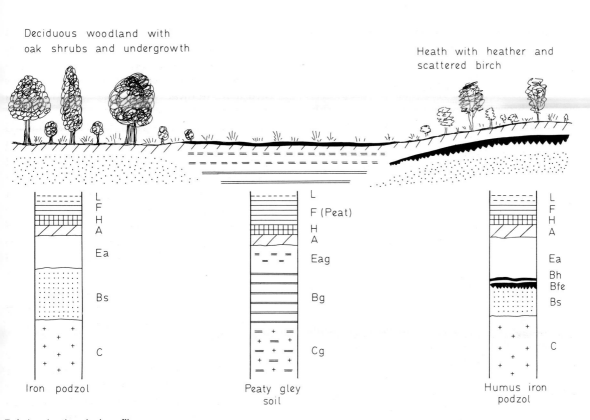

Deciduous woodland with oak shrubs and undergrowth

Heath with heather and scattered birch

Iron podzol	Peaty gley soil	Humus iron podzol
L F H A Ea Bs C	L F (Peat) H A Eag Bg Cg	L F H A Ea Bh Bfe Bs C

7.4 Lowland podzol profiles

Eag	0–17 cm.	Very dark grey-brown sandy loam with coarse sub-angular blocky peds; numerous well-weathered stones; few fissures or pores; abundant fine roots
Bh/Bfe	13–14 cm.	Soft 0.25 cm. layer of very dark brown organic-rich material overlies a strongly cemented 0.25 cm. iron pan; marked concentration of fine roots at the top of the pan
Bs	14–28 cm.	Strong brown gravelly loam; numerous stones up to 8 cm. diam.; friable; weakly cemented, breaking to crumb and fine sub-angular blocky peds; frequent fine roots
C	28 cm. +	Dark grey-brown gravelly sandy loam; weakly cemented; no fissures; but abundant pores; roots common; some dead; at 45 cm. the horizon merges into a loose, extremely stony layer (After Mackney and Burnham)

7.5 Diagrammatic profile of a peaty gleyed podzol

L
F Thin peat
H
A Thin organic and mineral horizon, strongly acid

Eag Bleached, gleyed and strongly acid eluvial horizon

Bh Strongly indurated iron pan with humus
Bfe accumulating above

Bs Orange-brown illuvial horizon enriched with iron, strongly acid

C Parent material, little altered sands and gravels or sandstones

There are difficulties in delimiting and classifying the soils which have minimal development of podzol features. Often the evidence of podzolization is shallow and easily destroyed by agriculture. As there is no real break between the podzols and the brown earths, some overlapping of the characters of both groups must be expected.

Brown podzolic soils

Brown podzolic soils (Alfic Ochrepts, Haplorthods; Leptic Podzols) were identified first in the New England area of the U.S.A. and the name has since been used in the British Isles. These soils lack an Ea horizon, but possess a B horizon which shows no increase in content of silicate clay. The B horizon is highly coloured in the upper part and this colour gradually fades with increasing depth (Plate 6). Whilst these soils are obviously closely related to the brown soils, a case can be made for retaining both brown soils and brown podzolic soils as separate items in classifications.

Profile of a brown podzolic soil (Haplorthod; Leptic Podzol), New York State, U.S.A.
(Parent material – glacial till and outwash material)

L, F, and H		Matted mor humus
A	0–2.5 cm.	Greyish-brown (10YR4/2) very fine sandy loam with weak fine crumb structure; very friable; white flecks of incipient eluvial horizon Ea may occur
Bs_1	2.5–20 cm.	Yellowish-brown (10YR5/6) very fine sand loam with weak medium crumb structure; friable; some stone fragments
Bs_2	20–45 cm.	Yellowish-brown (10YR5/4) very fine sandy loam with weak medium crumb structure; friable; some stone fragments.
Bs_3	45–65 cm.	Light yellowish-brown (10YR6/4) fine sandy loam or loam with weak course crumb structure; friable; some stone fragments
C	65–200 cm.	Pale brown (10YR6/3) to light brownish-grey (10YR6/2) silt loam or loam with moderate numbers of gravel and stone fragments; weakly coarse platy; firm to very firm and moderately compact in place; large roots penetrate this horizon

(After U.S.D.A.)

Soils of similar nature have been identified over extensive areas of sloping land in the western parts of Britain and Europe where names such as *podzolized sol brun acide* and *sol brun ocreux* have been used. In these regions, slope soils developed upon hard Palaeozoic sediments are often the only freely drained soils in a landscape dominated by peaty gley soils (Fragiochrepts; Dystric Gleysols) or upland gley podzols (Placaquods; Placic Podzols) (Fig. 7.6). The latter group of soils, like the ground-water podzols (Haplaquods; Gleyic Podzols) of the lowlands, has its lower horizons affected by the presence of water. In addition, the presence of an acid peaty humus together with bleached sand grains and gleying in the Eag horizon distinguishes these soils from other poorly drained upland soils.

Table 7.2 *Sub-groups and horizon sequence of podzol soils*

Sub-groups	Horizon sequence
Lowland:	
Iron-podzol	L F H A Ea Bs C
Humus-podzol	L F H A Ea Bh C
Humus-iron-podzol	L F H A Ea Bh Bfe Bs C
Ground-water podzol	L F H A Ea Bh/Bsg Cg
Upland:	
Brown podzolic	L F H A Bs C
Peaty gleyed podzol	Peat Ag Eag Bfe Bs C
Gley podzol	Peat Ag Eag Bsg Cg

Brown soils and argillic brown soils (Cambisols and Luvisols)

The brown soils are genetically related to the podzols, and in the sense that they are all leached soils, they were previously described as *podzolic*. It is important to note the usage of the word podzolic, for it describes soils which are by no means fully developed podzols. These soils are evenly distributed amongst the five continents and cover about 7 per cent of the land surface of the world (Fig. 11.1). The name *brown earth* was translated from Braunerde, the name given by the German scientist Ramann to soils of a uniform brown colour, lacking the distinctive horizons of the podzol, and occurring in central Europe. *Brown forest soils* were originally described in Europe as being developed under oak or beech forest, and their descriptions usually stress a calcareous

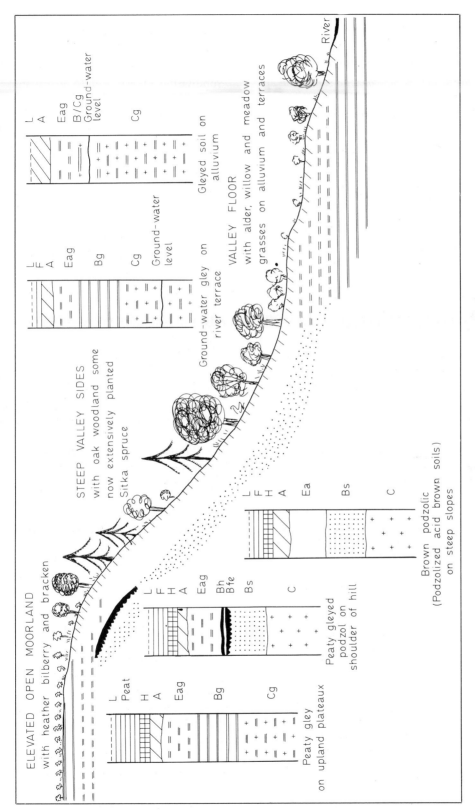

7.6 Upland podzol profiles

parent material. *Grey-brown podzolic* was the name given in the U.S.A. to describe soils with a thin litter horizon and a brown blocky B horizon of illuvial clay accumulation, whilst similar soils in Russia are called *derno-podzolic soils*. The approach adopted by French and Belgian pedologists in the classification of brown soils has found considerable support in Britain and elsewhere, so this account will follow their lead. Two basic soils are recognised beneath mull humus, these are the brown soils and the argillic brown soils.

The brown soils are characterised by having a weathered or *cambic B horizon* in which there has been significant change from the parent material in respect of colours, structure and removal of carbonates but insignificant amounts of illuvial clay, iron, aluminium or humus have accumulated (Fig. 7.7). Subdivision of the brown soils can be made into sandy soils of low base status developed on hard sandstones, and soils of higher base status and loamy texture from a variety of parent materials. The former group of soils are referred to as acid brown soils (Dystrochrepts; Dystric Cambisols), and the latter, more fertile soils, are simply called brown soils or brown earths (Eutrochrepts; Eutric Cambisols).

The argillic brown soils have as their major characteristic the development of an *argillic B horizon*. This is defined as having significantly more (illuvial) clay than the overlying horizons within limits that vary with texture. (In a loamy sand there must be a 3 per cent increase in clay, a sandy clay loam must have at least 1.2 times the

amount of clay in the E horizon and a clay soil must have at least 8 per cent more clay.) Usually these additional amounts of illuvial clay can be seen with a hand lens as clay skins on ped faces. Subdivision of the argillic brown soils (Alfisols; Orthic Luvisols) gives a group of weakly argillic brown soils, formerly called leached brown earths, which are transitional to brown soils and are common in central and southeast England. Other forms of argillic brown soils occur which are transitional to hydromorphic soils as well as the central concept with a strongly formed argillic B horizon which is commonly found in the Paris basin (Fig. 7.8).

Traditionally, a typical brown earth should possess the following salient features. It should be leached of carbonates, although some may be present in the C horizon or as added lime, and as a result it should be neutral to moderately acid (pH 4.5–6.5) with the base saturation and pH increasing with depth from the surface. The humus material should be of the mull type, although this may range from calcareous mull to acid mull or even moder in some soils transitional to the podzol group. The composition of the clay fraction should be constant throughout the profile as shown by the silica : sesquioxide ratio. The profile should be freely drained, although transitional forms of the gley group do occur.

In Europe and North America the parent materials of these soils are very variable as they are frequently formed from the deposits left after the Pleistocene Glaciations. South of the extent of the glacial deposits brown earths are

7.7 Diagrammatic profile of an acid brown soil

	L+F	Moder or acid mull humus
	A	Mixed mineral and organic horizon, strongly acid
	A/Bw	Transitional horizon, probably depleted by leaching
	Bw	Weathered horizon without appreciable enrichment with colloidal material discerned by slight differences of structure and colour
	C	Little altered sandstone, siltstone or glacial sand

7.8 Diagrammatic profile of an argillic brown soil

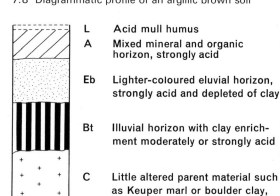

	L	Acid mull humus
	A	Mixed mineral and organic horizon, strongly acid
	Eb	Lighter-coloured eluvial horizon, strongly acid and depleted of clay
	Bt	Illuvial horizon with clay enrichment moderately or strongly acid
	C	Little altered parent material such as Keuper marl or boulder clay, possibly calcareous

characteristically found on sandstones, siltstones, clay and loess.

Brown earths and related soils are associated with those areas of the world's land surface originally covered with deciduous forest. In Europe these forests are characterised by oak, beech and ash woodlands, and in America by oak, beech, maple and hickory. Although now largely cleared, these forests originally had a canopy formed by the dominant trees and a rich undergrowth of smaller trees, herbs and grasses.

The climate in which these soils develop is not as extreme as that of the podzol zone to the north, and corresponds to the Köppen types, marine west coast (Cfb) and humid coastal climates (Dfa, Dfb, Dw, Dwb). Winter temperatures average about 0°C for less than three months of the year, and summer temperatures rarely exceed the range of 21–26 °C. Rainfall is evenly distributed throughout the year with a maximum occurring during the autumn months. Continued drought is rare. The amount of water received by the soil is sufficient to cause a moderate amount of leaching, but not enough to cause podzolization.

With the annual leaf-fall of the deciduous trees and the contribution from the smaller shrubs, herbs and grasses, the litter produced is more varied than that of the coniferous forest or heath. It is also of a higher nutritive status and is more easily digested by the soil-living fauna, which are present in greater numbers than in podzol soils. An efficient breakdown of plant tissue results. The humus is incorporated into the soil by the action of earthworms which drag material into their burrows from the surface, and ingest a mixture of mineral and organic matter. In their digestive tract, the mineral and organic matter is brought into very close association and when defecated comes to form mull humus. Therefore, the brown earth profile frequently lacks the superficial horizons of organic material other than the current year's leaf-fall. However, forms transitional to the podzol have acid mull, or even moder, where some superficial accumulation of organic material occurs. The A horizon is enriched by the presence of organic matter to between 3 and 5 per cent by weight in woodland soils. Most brown earths are used extensively for agriculture, the original forest having long since been cleared.

Brown soils

In Britain, the brown soils have been adopted as a major group within which the brown earths and the argillic brown earths are important groups together with brown calcareous soils and brown alluvial soils (see pp. 58, 62). This is in line with the original concepts proposed as a result of work in France and Belgium and allows comparison with the U.S. Soil Taxonomy and F.A.O./U.N.E.S.C.O. systems of classification (Table 7.1).

Typical brown earths (Eutrochrepts; Eutric Cambisols) in lowland Britain can be found on a wide range of parent materials including sandstones, shales and a variety of unconsolidated superficial deposits of Pleistocene age. All free calcium carbonate has been leached from the profile but calcium still dominates the exchangeable bases and the base status of these soils is considerably higher than that found in acid brown soils. The textures of typical brown earths are normally loamy, and although acid in the surface horizons, pH rises with depth until the parent material is reached which may or may not be calcareous.

Profile of a brown earth (Eutrochrept; Eutric Cambisol) from Somerset, England
(Parent material – Lower Lias limestone)

A 0– 8 cm. Dark brown (10YR3/4) humose loam with crumb structure; very friable; abundant roots; numerous earthworms; merging boundary

A/B 8–32 cm. Brown (7.5YR4/4) clay loam; occasional fragments of white limestone; sub-angular blocky structure; friable; organic matter following worm channels; numerous roots; merging boundary

B 32–57 cm. Brown to reddish brown (5YR to 7.5YR4/4) clay loam; fewer stones; sub-angular blocky structure; occasional roots; friable; clear boundary

C 57–80 cm. Weathering flaggy limestone with matrix of brown (7.5YR4/4) clay loam; firm; no organic matter; rare roots; abrupt boundary

R 80 cm. + Massive limestone

(After Findlay)

Typical acid brown soils (Dystrochrepts; Dystric Cambisols) in Britain and western Europe develop on hard, base-deficient rocks such as sandstones and siltstones or coarse-grained igneous rocks (Plate 7). These soils were first recognized as a separate sub-group in the Ardennes region. They lack any illuvial horizon with an accumulation of clay, iron or dispersed humus, but have a weathered B horizon which is distinguished by its structure and sometimes by its slightly brighter colour. These soils are strongly acid, pH 4.5, and have a low base content, which led to their original British name of 'brown earths of low base status'. Clay content is usually less than 20 per cent. There is a greater tendency for organic matter to form L and F horizons of the moder type in these acid soils. The mineral soil below is humus stained for 5 to 8 cm., to form the A horizon below which a transitional horizon can be distinguished. The weathered B horizon, indicated by Bw or (B), frequently has a brighter reddish or orange coloration, which gradually reduces in intensity with depth, eventually the C horizon is reached at about 50 cm. (Fig. 7.7 and Table 7.2).

Profile of an acid brown soil (Dystrochrept; Dystric Cambisol) from Carhaix, Finistère
(Parent material – fine-grained acid schists)

A	0.25 cm.	Grey-brown silt loam, stony with crumb and black structures, porous
A/B	25–33 cm.	Brown, slightly more clay than above, blocky structure
(B)	33–45 cm.	Slightly more ochreous, mixed pebbles of weathering schist and blocky fine earth
C	45 cm. +	Weathered schist material
		(After Aubert)

Argillic brown soils
Strongly developed argillic brown earths were called sols lessivés (Alfisols; Orthic Luvisols) in France where their parent materials were decalcified medium- or fine-textured weathered residue from sedimentary rocks, loess, plateau drifts, ancient alluvia or glacial till. Following the removal of lime, it would appear that bases are leached from the exchange positions leading to an increase in acidity. As the depth of leached soil increases and the flocculating effect of the calcium ions is reduced, a gradual movement of clay particles begins. These are washed (lessivé) from the A and Eb horizons into the Bt horizon where

the clay particles are deposited on and lie parallel to the ped faces. By this means the Bt horizon gradually has its clay content increased and comes to have a well-developed medium prismatic or blocky structure which contrasts with the weaker blocky structures of the Eb and A horizons. The clay is not broken down chemically but particles are washed down the pores and cracks in the soil, particularly after the period of summer drying when shrinkage cracks are most evident (Figs. 4.3 and 4.4).

Although these soils can be seen in the British Isles, the conditions of mainland Europe show increasing continentality which seems to encourage their development. The feature of an argillic horizon is a characteristic which these soils share with the former grey-brown podzolic soils (Udalfs) of the U.S.A. and the derno-podzolic soils of the U.S.S.R. (Table 7.2).

Profile of a sol lessivé (Alfisol; Luvisol) from the Paris region
(Parent material – Loess overlying sandstone)

A	0– 7 cm.	Very dark brown (7.5YR2/2) silt loam with weak crumb structure many roots
Eb	7– 21 cm.	Yellowish-brown (10YR5/4) silt, moderately well-developed blocky structure; many roots gradual boundary
Bt_1	21– 65 cm.	Light yellowish-brown (10YR6/4) silt with well-developed blocky structure; common roots; irregular boundary
Bt_2	67– 97 cm.	Yellowish-brown (10YR6/4) silty clay with medium and fine blocky structure well developed brown (7.5YR4/4) clay skins (1 mm.), numerous and obvious roots common, clear boundary
C_1	97–112 cm.	Loess in which some cracks are filled with clay
C/D	112–180 cm.	Pale brown loess overlying gritstone
		(After Federoff)

On pervious parent materials such as loess these soils remain freely drained, but it will be appreciated that the Bt horizon with fewer cracks, and these partially infilled with clay, can present an impedance to water moving down the profile. Therefore, on clayey materials with level sites, and particularly on older landscapes (p. 56), or where lateral seepage occurs, features of gleying are apparent (Plates 9 and 29). Thus the brown soils and soils with argillic horizons may merge laterally into analogous soils with gleying, or even surface-water gley soils depending upon the intensity of gleying conditions at any given site.

Weakly argillic brown earths of Britain and sols bruns lessivés of France (Typic Hapludalfs; Orthic Luvisols), in which the clay migration to the B horizon is not so pronounced, constitute a second group of the argillic brown soils. These soils are developed extensively in central and eastern England on fine loamy parent materials. It would appear that the development of argillic B horizons becomes stronger as conditions become more continental. Soils with well developed Bt horizons are not common in Britain but movement of clay from the Eb horizon can be demonstrated in many soils by micromorphological studies of soil fabric and by comparison of the clay contents of eluvial and illuvial horizons. Usually the Eb horizon of these soils can be discerned by its lighter colour and weaker, coarser structure (Fig. 7.8 and Plate 8). The example below from Britain gives the salient features of

these soils. It can be considered as belonging to a transitional group of soils between true brown soils with cambic B horizons and those with argillic B horizons.

Profile of an argillic brown soil (Hapludalf; Orthic Luvisol) from Shropshire, England
(Parent material – Devonian marl)

Ap	0–20 cm.	Dark reddish-brown stoneless silt loam; fine and medium sub-angular blocky structure; friable; permeable; easily penetrated by roots
Eb	20–30 cm.	Reddish-brown stoneless silt loam; medium sub-angular blocky structure; friable; permeable; easily penetrated by roots
Bt	30–75 cm.	Somewhat brighter reddish-brown stoneless silty clay loam with prismatic structure breaking to coarse angular blocky; compact; plastic, not easily penetrated by water and roots except along cracks
C	75 cm. +	Bright reddish-brown marl, often blotched with grey-green; angular blocky or platy structure; more permeable; often calcareous below about 120 cm.

(After Mackney and Burnham)

7.9 Diagrammatic section of Lowland Britain from near Leicester to the North Sea indicating relationship between soils and parent materials

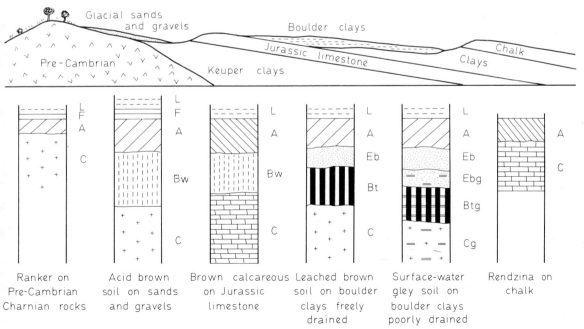

Ranker on Pre-Cambrian Charnian rocks

Acid brown soil on sands and gravels

Brown calcareous on Jurassic limestone

Leached brown soil on boulder clays freely drained

Surface-water gley soil on boulder clays poorly drained

Rendzina on chalk

As clay eluviation is such a distinctive feature, some pedologists are reluctant to include soils with cambic and argillic horizons in the same category. The original definiton of a brown earth does not include any mention of clay movement and it would seem sensible to draw the dividing line between brown soils and argillic brown soils in a similar position to that between Inceptisols and Alfisols of Soil Taxonomy.

Variations such as the *rendzina* (Plate 28) and *ranker* occur within the brown earth zone of soil formation (Fig. 7.9) together with brown calcareous soils and the gley soils mentioned previously. The influence of parent material plays a fairly strong part in deciding the type of soil produced. These soils will be described more fully in the chapter on intrazonal and azonal soils.

Grey soils

These soils are formed in a more continental environment between the podzol and the chernozem zones of soil formation in North America and in Russia (Fig. 11.1). The climate in which these soils have been formed has mean annual temperatures of $-9\ ^{\circ}C$ in January and $19\ ^{\circ}C$ in July. Precipitation is light, 550 mm. per annum, and 45 per cent of it falls as early summer rain. These are average figures for European Russia. There is a variation from east to west with both rainfall and length of frost-free period increasing westwards. Similar climatic conditions exist in the North American districts where these soils occur. Climatologically, this zone is described by Thornthwaite as 'subhumid and semi-arid microthermal climate' and by Köppen as 'humid continental with short summers' (Dfb, Dwb). Conditions suitable for the development of these soils do not occur in the southern hemisphere.

The parent materials of Canadian grey wooded soils (Eutroboralfs, Cryoboralfs; Albic Luvisols and Podzoluvisols) in Alberta and Saskatchewan are calcareous tills, lacustrine and outwash material of Late Glacial Age. Similar parent materials occur in U.S.S.R. such as loess-like loams and glacial deposits upon which the derno-podzolic soils (Glossudalfs, Glossoboralfs; Podzoluvisols) are developed. These soils are associated with the northern part of the transition from forest to steppeland northeast of Moscow where there is a spruce, pine, and oak forest with birch,

and they also occur west of Lake Superior in Northern Wisconsin and Minnesota.

The profile of these soils resembles that of the podzol with a thin raw humus horizon (5 cm.). The A horizon is not always well developed and a pronounced platy Ea horizon tongues into the Bt horizon which has well developed clay skins and coatings of organic matter. As these soils have the superficial morphology of a podzol in the upper part of the profile and an argillic B horizon they have been called Podzoluvisols on the F.A.O./U.N.E.S.C.O. Soil Map of the World. The chief difference between the Albic Luvisols and Podzoluvisols appears to be a lower base saturation in the argillic B horizon of the Podzoluvisols. An example of a derno-podzolic soil from Yaroslavl is given below to illustrate these soils.

Profile of a derno-podzolic soil (Glossoboralf; Podzoluvisol) Yaroslavl, U.S.S.R.
(Parent material – loess-like loams over moraine)

L	0– 1 cm.	Litter of weakly decomposed leaves
F	1– 2 cm.	Dark brown (10YR3/2) moderately decomposed plant material with occasional bleached quartz grains; clear wavy boundary
A_1	2– 11 cm.	Very dark grey (10YR3/1) with numerous mottles; sandy loam with weak fine crumb structure; abundant roots; abrupt wavy boundary
A_2	11– 27 cm.	Brown (10YR5/3) with numerous mottles, sandy loam with weak platy structure; common roots; brown and black concretions; earthworms; abrupt wavy boundary
$A2_2$	27– 42 cm.	Pale brown (10YR6/3) with numerous mottles; sandy loam with weak thin platy structure; many hard round concretions; abrupt irregular boundary
A/B	42– 60 cm.	Transitional horizon of light brownish grey (10YR6/2) tonguing down vertical fissures into a brown (7.5YR4/4) sandy loam with sub-angular blocky structure; irregular boundary

2

4

Stone stripes, Iceland. Regular freeze-thaw cycles have separated material of different sizes into parallel lines, a feature found particularly on sloping ground. **2 Humus-iron podzol,** Norfolk, U.K. This profile is developed in acid, freely drained sands and gravels beneath a 'heath' type of vegetation. Eluvial and illuvial horizons are clearly seen. **3 Humus podzol,** Drenthe, Holland. This profile is developed in dune sands lacking in iron, consequently only a Bh horizon develops. Multiple profiles have developed where further sand has accumulated. **4 Gley podzol,** Lincolnshire, U.K. Poorly drained conditions cause the mottled appearance with areas of weakly cemented orange-brown sand. The surface soil is rich in organic matter and the profile has developed in blown sand.

5 **Peaty gleyed podzol,** Breconshire, U.K. Higher rainfall and peaty tendency cause poor drainage in surface horizons of soil. A thin, often convoluted, iron pan develops below which the soil is freely drained. 6 **Brown podzolic soil,** Glamorganshire, U.K. Enriched by humus in the surface horizon, these soils lack an eluvial Ea horizon. The B horizon is highly coloured and the soil is developed on sloping sites on acid parent materials. 7 **Acid brown soil,** Derbyshire, U.K. The profile is developed upon base-deficient parent materials a does not show any evidence of accumulation of clay or of ir or humus in the (B) horizon. 8 **Leached brown soil,** Derb shire, U.K. Developed from fine-grained, slightly calcareo parent material, these soils are first leached, then moveme of clay into the Bt horizon begins.

Brown earth with gleying, Nottinghamshire, U.K. Super-imposed upon the features of a leached brown soil are the pale colours indicative of slow drainage. **10 Grey forest soil, U.S.S.R.** The development of a pronounced illuvial horizon by clay and humus movement has left the A horizon structures with a coating of fine silica grains which give the grey colour. **Red Mediterranean soil,** Toledo Province, Spain. Dev-eloped from Silurian shales, this profile has the pronounced reddened, clay-enriched Bt horizon typical of these soils. **12 Red-brown earth,** Barossa Valley, South Australia. These soils are characterised by a red-brown surface soil below which is a darker, clay-enriched Bt horizon the lower parts of which are calcareous.

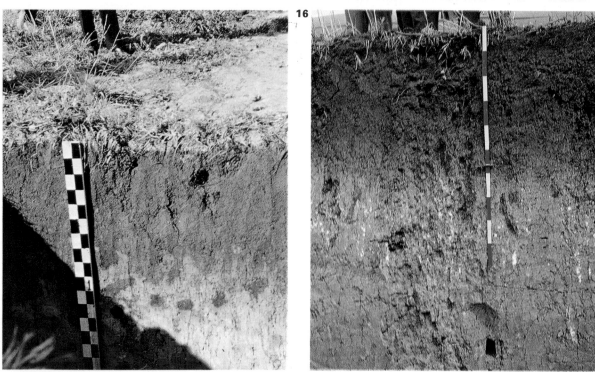

13 Calcareous concretion, South Australia. The lower horizon has become impregnated with a rock-like accumulation of calcium carbonate (the knife rests upon it). Erosion of the overlying soil exposes the 'crust' of calcium carbonate at the surface. **14 Yellow podzolic soil,** N.S.W., Australia. Strongly weathered and leached profile develops in low-lying situations in the landscape where moister conditions prevail. **15 Chernozem,** U.S.S.R. The deep humus-rich A horizon of this 'typical' chernozem is about 1 m. in depth. Krotovinas ca[n] be seen in the lighter-coloured C horizon. The horizon [of] accumulation of calcium carbonate Cca, deeper in the pi[t] cannot be seen here. **16 Southern chernozem,** U.S.S.[R.] The A horizon is not so deep nor so rich in humus as in th[e] 'typical' chernozem. Note the calcium carbonate accumulatio[n] in the C horizon.

17 **Chestnut soil,** U.S.S.R. Drier conditions and less organic matter give these shallow soils a lighter colour. The calcium carbonate accumulation is closer to the surface as leaching is less effective. **18 Desert soil,** N.S.W., Australia. Formed from mineral material and lacking in organic matter, this soil is little more than an accumulation of alluvial material washed from adjacent higher ground. **19 Ferrallitic soil,** Misuku, Africa. Freely drained sites in the humid tropical regions develop deep red soils which are acid in reaction. Silica is removed from the clay minerals. Quartz is relatively stable. Iron and aluminium sesquioxides may form a substantial part of the mineral matter. **20 Yellow latosol,** Queensland, Australia. In moister situations yellow iron compounds are formed. Other characteristics are similar to those of red ferrallitic soils.

21 Vertisol, N.S.W., Australia. The lowest parts of the landscape in tropical and sub-tropical areas have dark coloured, base-rich soils with montmorillonitic clays. **22 Gilgai,** Narrabri, N.S.W., Australia. The physical properties of the clay in these soils enables them to crack widely. Material falls down the cracks, and the soil gradually inverts itself. It also is forced into humps and hollows with an amplitude of 1 to 2 metres.

23 Krasnozem, Childers Plateau, Queensland, Australia. Deep, friable, red, loamy soils developed from base-rich parent materials occur in the sub-tropics. As the high iron content restricts eluvial movement, horizon development is not obvious. **24 Pisolitic laterite,** Victoria Point, Queensland, Australia. Lateritic concretions can take the form of rounded nodules consisting mainly of iron oxides.

25 **Slag-like laterite,** Victoria Point, Queensland, Australia. Hardening of the iron oxides in the mottled horizon has given rise to this slag-like deposit. 26 **Lateritic crust,** York, Western Australia. The irreversible hardening of the iron oxides in the soil as they are dried gives rise to an indurated crust after the material above has been eroded. 27 **Laterite** exposure, York, Western Australia. Erosion has left laterite cappings to the interfluves in the York area of Western Australia. The ironstone crust and pallid horizon can be seen clearly. 28 **Rendzina,** Transylvania Alps, Romania. Shallow, humus-rich soils over calcareous parent materials are referred to as rendzinas.

29 Gley soil, Derbyshire, U.K. Poorly drained conditions in the soil cause chemical reduction of iron compounds; mottling with grey and orange colours are typical. **30 Solonchak,** Buzau, Romania. An alluvial soil which has become salinized. This detailed photograph shows pores and channels in the soil filled with white salts. Efflorescences of salts also occur on the surface of the soil. **31 Solonetz,** U.S.S.R. Partly leached of salts, this soil profile demonstrates the rounded tops of the columnar structures associated with solonetz. The topsoil shows a distinct lack of structure. **32 Peat,** Breconshire, U.K. On upland, high rainfall areas in western Britain, accumulation of peat has been encouraged to form the 'blanket bog'. These organic soils have developed upon acid shales with strong gleying conditions in the mineral material beneath.

B1	60–87 cm.	Reddish brown (5YR4/4) fine sandy loam with massive, breaking easily to sub-angular blocky structure, gradual wavy boundary
B2t	87–140 cm.	Brown (10YR4/4) with light grey mottles; loam with prismatic structure; dark brown clay skins; gradual wavy boundary
B2tg	140–167 cm.	Brown (7.5YR5/4) with light grey mottles; loam with prismatic structure; few black concentrations; gradual boundary
B3tg	167–207 cm.	Yellowish brown (10YR5/4) mottled with greyish brown (10YR5/2) clay loam with coarse prismatic structure
IIB IIID	207–298 cm.	Layers transitional from mantle loam to sandy loam of moraine below

(After Targulian *et al.*)

Grey forest soils (Argiborolls; Orthic grey-zems) are associated with the southern part of the transition from forest to steppeland. The forest of these regions has been cleared from extensive areas, but originally it was a broad-leaf forest of oak, lime, maple, birch and hazel in Europe, and poplar, spruce, fir, larch and ponderosa pine in North America. On the forest floor was a grassy herbaceous cover. Litter from this diverse plant cover has been incorporated into the soil in a mull form of humus.

7.10 Diagrammatic profile of a grey forest soil

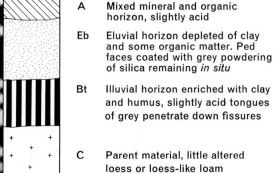

	L	Mull humus
	A	Mixed mineral and organic horizon, slightly acid
	Eb	Eluvial horizon depleted of clay and some organic matter. Ped faces coated with grey powdering of silica remaining *in situ*
	Bt	Illuvial horizon enriched with clay and humus, slightly acid tongues of grey penetrate down fissures
	C	Parent material, little altered loess or loess-like loam

Profile of a grey forest soil (Argiboroll, Orthic Greyzem) from near Tula, U.S.S.R.
(Parent material – non-calcareous loess overlying morainic material)

A	0–15 cm.	Dark grey clayey soil with fine nutty structure; friable; compact root mat; even boundary
A/Eb	15–40 cm.	Dark grey clayey soil (lighter when dry) with medium to coarse nutty structure; fewer roots; organic material coating peds, boundary tongues into horizon below
Eb	40–60 cm.	Brownish-grey clayey soil with pallid powdering on ped faces; prismatic-nutty structure; compact wavy boundary
Bt	60–110 cm.	Greyish-brown clayey soil with prismatic structure, more compact than horizon above; bright coatings upon ped faces
Bt/C	110–190 cm.	Brown to bright brown clayey soil with blocky to prismatic structures; coatings upon ped faces; uneven boundary. Reddish-brown sandy loam morainic material

(After Fridland)

The results of the soil-forming processes reflect some features of neighbouring zones. Leaching occurs to a lesser extent than it does in the brown earth soils, while evidence of calcification in the B horizon resembles that of the chernozems. The amount and the form of the humus of the grey forest soils resembles that of the leached chernozems or prairie soils. A feature of the grey forest soils, already seen in the leached soils, is the removal of clay from the upper horizons to form a Bt horizon with clay skins, indicating a process which is absent in the true chernozem soil. The grey colour of the A horizon is caused by the powdering of fine grains of silica remaining on the ped faces, following removal of clay to the lower horizons (Fig. 7.10 and Plate 10).

It would seem that the soils of the grey forest soil group have developed under changing biotic conditions. Profile evidence from the region of Kursk indicates that these soils may have developed under steppe conditions. Subsequently they became wooded and leaching resulted aided by a slight climatic change which encouraged tree growth. The presence of krotovinas, infilled burrows of steppe-living animals, in the grey forest soils as well as in the chernozems, seems to substantiate this view. The description of a representative profile from near Tula illustrates the features of these soils.

From their geographical position and the previous comments it will be appreciated that these grey soils have formed in areas of gradual transition. As a result their distribution is discontinuous depending upon the interplay of the factors of soil formation. The horizon sequences at these grey soils and the brown soils are given in Table 7.3.

Table 7.3 *Sub-groups and horizon sequence of Brown and Grey Soils*

Sub-groups	Horizon sequence			
Brown soils	A	A/B	Bw	C
Argillic brown soils	A	Eb	Bt	C
Grey wooded soils	A	Ea	Bt	C
Grey forest soils	A	Eb	Bt	C

8 SOILS OF THE MID-LATITUDES, WARM CLIMATES

Soil development in the mid-latitudes is conditioned by a wide range of climates with many transitional zones and variations. However, mid-latitude climates can be divided into four main categories allowing soil formation to be considered within these as a framework. They are the 'Mediterranean' areas, humid sub-tropical or southeast coastal margins, temperate continental areas and the deserts.

The main soils of the warm temperate parts of the world are summarised in Table 8.1 which gives the common names and synonyms of soils in the U.S. Soil Taxonomy and the F.A.O./U.N.E.S.C.O. World Soil Map Legend.

Soils of the Mediterranean areas

In those parts of the world which experience mild, moist winters and warm, dry summers, the vegetation and soil response is typified by that in the Mediterranean Basin. Similar environments occurring in California, southern and western Australia, South Africa and Chile are classified by Köppen as Cs climates. The zonal soils formed are brown earths, brown and red Mediterranean soils, and cinnamon soils (Fig. 11.1). In terms of modern classifications these are mainly varieties of soil with cambic or argillic B horizons, thereby qualifying as Inceptisols or Alfisols of the U.S. Soil Taxonomy or Cambisols and Luvisols of the F.A.O. U.N.E.S.C.O. World Soil Map Legend.

Winter temperatures between 5 °C and 15 °C are characteristic of Mediterranean lands. The rainfall of about 500 mm. per annum is derived from depressions which develop over the sea during the cooler season. The soils are thoroughly moistened by this rain, only to be parched again during the ensuing summer which is characterised by little or no rainfall and temperatures between 25 °C and 30 °C. The length of the

Table 8.1 *Synonyms for soils of the warm temperate regions*

Common names	U.S. Soil Taxonomy	F.A.O./U.N.E.S.C.O. World Map Legend
Mediterranean areas		
Brown Mediterranean soils	Hapludalfs	Orthic Luvisols
Red Mediterranean soils }	Rhodustalfs	Chromic Luvisols
Red brown earths		
Non-calcic brown soils	Haploxeralfs	Orthic Luvisols
Cinnamon soils	Ustochrepts	Chromic Luvisols
Warm Temperate East Coast Margin areas		
Red podzolic soils	Fragiudults	Plinthic Acrisols
Yellow podzolic soils	Paleudults	Orthic Acrisols
Continental Interior areas		
Chernozems	Udolls; Ustolls	Chernozems
Prairie soils	Udolls	Phaeozems
Chestnut soils	Ustolls	Kastanozems
Desert and Semi-desert areas		
Sierozems	Aridisols	Xerosols
Raw mineral soils	Entisols	Yermosols

summer drought appears to be an important factor in the formation of soils in this region. Increasing length of drought produces a sequence of soils ranging from brown earths developing in a leaching environment with less than one month summer drought, to the cinnamon soils where five or six months' drought leads to a calcification type of soil formation transitional to that of the continental interiors. Between these two extremes the red and brown Mediterranean soils are formed.

The vegetation of the Mediterranean lands originally appears to have been an evergreen forest of broadleaved and coniferous trees, in particular various species of oak and pines. Many years of human intervention have removed much of this forest by lumbering, burning and grazing. A secondary growth known as *maquis* on non-calcareous soils and *garrigue* on calcareous soils has developed as a sub-climax vegetation. Removal of the original forest initiated soil erosion over large areas.

The parent materials from which these soils are formed in Europe consist of sandstones, shales and particularly limestones and calcareous marls. The two latter are common south of the Alps. As considerable erosion has occurred there has been redistribution of the parent materials

A   Mull humus
Eb   Eluvial horizon which has lost clay. Slightly acid
Bt/ir   Illuvial horizons which are
Bir/C   enriched with clay and iron and have become red-coloured
C   Limestone or calcareous marl

8.1 Diagrammatic profile of a brown Mediterranean soil

leaving rocky hills with thick colluvial accumulations in the valleys and hollows of the landscape. This redistribution is common in older landscapes, particularly in semi-arid areas such as Australia, which have been land areas for long periods of geological history. This leads to a complicated soil pattern with old soils lying adjacent to immature ones upon the same landscape. In southern Europe, northern Africa and parts of Australia deep red clays known as terra rossa have accumulated from the weathering of the limestones of karst areas to form a distinctive parent material for soil formation.

8.2 Mediterranean soils and relationship to landscape

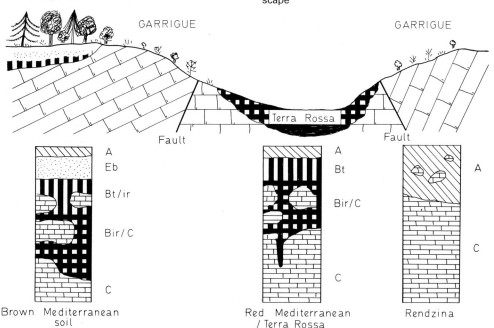

FOREST   GARRIGUE   GARRIGUE

Terra Rossa

Fault   Fault

A
Eb
Bt/ir
Bir/C
C

Brown Mediterranean soil

A
Bt
Bir/C
C

Red Mediterranean / Terra Rossa

A
C

Rendzina

Brown Mediterranean soils (Hapludalfs; Orthic Luvisols) represent a natural continuation of the Brown soils of cooler climates. Formed from non-calcareous or decalcified parent materials they are characterised by a brown colour, a friable humus-rich A horizon and a denser and less friable argillic B horizon (Fig. 8.1). Where these soils have developed on calcareous parent materials, the upper horizons have been decalcified and clay movement has occurred. In the lower part of the illuvial horizon, and on the linings of fissures in the C horizon, clay has been redeposited in calcareous conditions as the soil dries during the hot, dry summer. At the same time siliceous-iron complexes are irreversibly precipitated to give the rich red colour of the lower horizons of these soils. This is a process of weak ferrallitization known as *rubefaction* which is even more important in tropical soils which have formed under a climate with a pronounced dry season (p. 33). It results in soils which are classified as Rhodustalfs or Calcic and Chromic Luvisols.

Profile of a brown Mediterranean soil (Hapludalf; Orthic Luvisol) from Rivier Sonder End, Cape Province, South Africa
(Parent material – schists)

Ap 0– 13 cm. Greyish-brown, crumbly to slightly loose gravelly sandy clay loam mixed with quartz grit and small angular shale fragments, humus deficient, but common roots in upper 10 cm. Material from B horizon has been incorporated by cultivation

B 13– 63 cm. Reddish-brown gravelly clay; crumbly when dry and fairly compact when wet; stones and gravel consist of hard angular shale fragments

C_1 63– 79 cm. Yellowish-brown, mottled reddish-brown partly weathered hard and soft shale with an appreciable amount of clay

C_2 79–150 cm. Slightly weathered greyish-brown shales, moderately soft
(After Van der Merwe)

Some of the red Mediterranean soils (Rhodustalfs) have resulted from soil formation in the eroded remains of these brown Mediterranean soils (Fig. 8.2 and Plate 11). Other red soils are formed upon the relic clays resulting from the weathering of the limestone. Often these soils occupy discontinuous pockets surrounded by rocky limestone outcrops. These soils are usually less than 1 m. in depth and, although derived from limestone by solution, are often slightly calcareous through enrichment by calcium-rich solutions from surrounding areas of limestone. Their profile usually comprises a dark red clay, somewhat enriched with organic matter, which has a friable consistence. Lower horizons are formed of a firm blocky clay which becomes very plastic when wet.

Profile of a red Mediterranean soil (Rhodustalf; Chromic Luvisol) from Tlemcen, Algeria
(Parent material – Jurassic Limestone)

A 0– 20 cm. Brown-red loam with coarse blocky structure, relatively hard consistence with numerous roots

B_1 20– 50 cm. Dark red clay with blocky structure, plastic consistence and numerous roots

B_2 50– 80 cm. Dark red clay with blocky structure, plastic consistence, common roots

C 80–160 cm. Red clay loam with blocky structure, ped surfaces glossy, plastic consistence, numerous calcareous nodules

R 160 cm. + Limestone
(After Durand)

Red-brown earths (Rhodustalfs; Chromic Luvisols) are described from the Barossa Valley of South Australia, an area which experiences a Mediterranean type of climate (Plate 12). These soils occur on a wide range of parent materials which are to be found between the 350 and

8.3 Diagrammatic profile of a red Mediterranean soil and terra rossa

A   Thin mull humus forming in eroded remains
Bt of B horizon

Bir/C Illuvial horizons which are enriched with clay and iron and have become red-coloured

C   Limestone or calcareous marls

630 mm. isohyets. As they are subjected to strong weathering, these red-brown earths have some clay eluviation from the upper part of the soil profile, with the deposition of clay and calcium carbonate in an argillic horizon. Movement of these constituents is dependent upon the seasonal rainfall which causes periodic saturation and downward percolation (Fig. 8.3).

Profile of a red-brown earth, (Rhodustalf; Chromic Luvisol) Barossa Valley, South Australia
(Parent material – Pleistocene colluvial deposits)

A_1 0– 8 cm. Light brown hard, compact and cemented loam

A_2 8– 15 cm. Light reddish-brown compact clay loam

B_1 15– 60 cm. Dark reddish-brown friable granular to granular nutty clay which becomes blocky in the lower part of the horizon

B_{ca} 60–135 cm. Dark reddish-brown clay with small amounts of lime

C 135 cm. + Mottled brown and reddish-brown clay continues to 300 cm.
(After C.S.I.R.O.)

The former group of non-calcic brown soils are rather similar to the red-brown earths, but they lack the calcareous B_{ca} horizon. Instead, the B horizon of the non-calcic brown soil can be distinguished by a prismatic structure and a change in texture. These soils are characteristic of the wheat belt of Western Australia and beneath mixed forest and grassland in the south-west United States.

8.4 Diagrammatic profile of a cinnamon soil

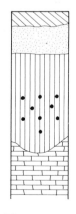

A   Mull humus. Mixed organic mineral horizon, neutral or slightly acid

Eb

Bca Undifferentiated B horizon, increasing clay content with depth, calcareous

C   Slightly calcareous clay parent material

Where a longer summer drought is experienced, the characteristics of the soils gradually become more typical of the drier, semi-arid steppelands. Light yellowish-brown soils result which Russian authors call *cinnamon soils* (Ustochrepts, Haploxeralfs; Chromic Cambisols, Chromic Luvisols). The general features of these soils are that they have a blocky structure and a clay content which increases from the lower part of the A horizon downwards through the profile (Fig. 8.4). Calcium carbonate concretions may occur below about 30 cm. in these soils in drier localities. The A horizon is reported to be moderately rich in organic matter, ranging between 4 and 7 per cent. These cinnamon soils occur in eastern Spain, the Balkans, Turkey, Central Asia, North Africa, as well as in California, Mexico, Chile, China and Australia. They are the zonal type which has developed in response to the drier type of Mediterranean climate.

Profile of a cinnamon brown soil (Haploxeralf; Chromic Luvisol) from Khasavyurta, Dhagestan
(Parent material – not given)

A_1 0– 10 cm. Cinnamon-brown with dark grey cast, silty-blocky, mellow, matted with roots. Does not effervesce. Gradual transition

A_2 10– 41 cm. Darker colour than above, prismoidal-blocky, somewhat compact. Does not effervesce. Gradual transition

B_1 41– 55 cm. Grey with a brown tone, prismoidal-blocky, somewhat compact. Contains pseudo-mycelium (p. 75). Fine clay loam, effervesces. Distinct transition

B_2 55– 75 cm. Dark pale-yellow with white spots. Blocky-lumpy compact contains large quantities of pseudo-mycelium. Fine clay loam effervesces vigorously to the end of the profile.

C_1 75–118 cm. Lighter colour than above, cloddy, compact, effloresces of carbonate medium clay loam

C_2 118–170 cm. Dark pale-yellow, cloddy, compact, carbonate in the form of spots and veins. Clay loam

C_3 170–265 cm. Dark pale-yellow, lumpy, compact, coarse clay loam
(After Zalibekov)

Various intrazonal soils also occur which deserve mention. On the many outcrops of limestone rocks in the Mediterranean Basin, rendzinas (Rendolls) occur with fine-textured, crumb-structured, calcareous shallow profiles. Similar shallow soils on clays and other non-calcareous parent material are termed *rankers* (Lithic Xerorthent). These are often associated with the higher and steeper mountainous areas. Hard layers of calcium carbonate (petrocalcic horizons) in soils are called calcrete but the name *croûte calcaire* is used in Algeria and *kafkalla* in Cyprus. Similar soils also occur in South Australia (Plate 13). These crusts were concretionary horizons originally formed by an accumulation of calcium carbonate within the soil profile which was subsequently revealed at the surface by erosion.

Poor drainage is not a characteristic generally associated with the soils of these regions for, although examples of gley soils do occur, most soils, even river alluvia, are not gleyed. Some alluvial soils may show signs of salt enrichment, particularly where salty waters have been used for irrigation in areas of less than 500 mm. annual rainfall. Seasonally poorly drained soils similar to the vertisols of the sub-tropical regions are reported from Morocco and other parts of North Africa. These soils, called *tirs* (Usterts or Xererts; Pellic Vertisols), are black or dark brown fine-textured clays which occupy the lower parts of the landscape.

Soils of the warm-temperate east coast margin climate

Occupying a similar position to the Mediterranean climates but on the eastern sides of the continental land masses are those areas which experience the warm-temperate east margin type of climate. The zonal soil type of this climate is that exemplified by the red and yellow podzolic soil (Ultisols; Acrisols). Features observed in these soils suggest the effects of strong leaching, whilst other features are suggestive of ferrallitization. Geographically, these soils occur in areas with warm, moist environments, midway between the main areas of podzolization and ferrallitization, so it is not surprising to find evidence of both processes present. The main areas where these soils can be seen are in the southeast of the United States, central China, eastern Australia and eastern Brazil (Fig. 11.1).

The climatic regime in which the red and yellow podzolic soils are formed is one of hot, humid summers with convective rainfall, and short mild winters with precipitation from frontal activity between air masses of different character. Rainfall is well distributed throughout the year, and amounts to between 1250 and 1500 mm. per annum. Average temperatures range from around 5 °C in the coldest month to about 25 °C in the summer. This climate is called humid sub-tropical (Cfa) by Köppen.

The deciduous forests which remain indicate a former cover composed of oak, hickory and chestnut on the freely drained upland areas. Low-lying, poorly drained land carried stands of slash and loblolly pine with cypress. Whilst these trees formed the canopy, they allowed sufficient light to penetrate through to the forest floor for a dense shrub and herbaceous under-storey to develop.

Granites, gneisses, schists, sandstones, shales, limestones and various unconsolidated sediments are quoted as parent materials for these soils in the United States. Most of these parent materials are well weathered, siliceous and situated upon geomorphologically old land surfaces which pre-date glaciation.

Red-yellow podzolic soils are defined as 'a group of well-developed, well-drained acid soils having thin organic and organic-mineral horizons over a light-coloured bleached horizon, over a red, yellowish-red or yellow, more clayey B horizon'. They are characterised by a bare saturation of less than 35 per cent and some weatherable minerals remain.

The moist climate throughout the year is conducive to strong leaching, and the evidence for this is seen in the acid surface horizons. A maximum amount of clay occurs deeper in the profile, but this seems to be caused for the most part by kaolinite formation *in situ* rather than by translocation of clay down the profile. The red and yellow colours of these soils indicate different degrees of hydration of the iron oxides; the red soils develop in drier conditions and the yellow where moister conditions prevail (Fig. 8.5 and Plate 14).

Profile of a red podzolic soil (Fragiudult; Plinthic Acrisol) from Virginia, U.S.A.
(Parent material – weathered gneiss)

A_{00}		Thin layer of leaves and pine needles
A_1	0– 5 cm.	Brownish-grey very friable sandy loam with fine weak crumb structure, strongly acid
A_2	5– 20 cm.	Weak yellow to light yellowish-brown nearly loose or very friable sandy loam, strongly acid
B_1	20– 25 cm.	Weak reddish-brown to strong brown friable sandy loam or lightly sandy clay loam with medium granular structure, strongly acid
B_2	25– 95 cm.	Moderate to strong reddish-brown clay, plastic when wet, very firm when moist and very hard when dry, medium blocky structure, some white sand grains and small mica flakes, strongly acid
B_3	95–150 cm.	Light to moderate reddish-brown clay loam with mottles of yellow, firm to friable when moist, weak coarse blocky structure with enough mica flakes to make it feel slippery, strongly acid
C	150 cm. +	Mottled light reddish-brown, yellowish-brown, light grey and black friable disintegrated rock material

(After U.S.D.A.)

Although the southeast of the U.S.A. is where most work has been done upon their development, these soils are not confined to this region. Similar soils are described from the U.S.S.R. in the state of Georgia where they occur on the shores of the Black and Caspian Seas, south of the main Caucasian ranges. In Australia, particularly in New South Wales, areas which experience 500 to 650 mm. rainfall per annum develop these soils. They occur extensively upon the elevated tablelands in the eastern part of the state, where they are developed upon Palaeozoic sediments. The red podzolic soils occur upon the freely drained interfluve sites, and the yellow podzolic soils occupy the lower sites in the land-

Profile of a yellow podzolic soil (Paleudult: Orthic Acrisol) from Cheltenham, near Sydney, Australia.
(Parent material – sandy shale)

A_1	0– 5 cm.	Grey to dark-brown (10YR5/1, to 10YR3/3), friable, crumb-structured loam or silt loam
A_2	5–25 cm.	Very pale brown to yellowish-brown (10YR7/4, to 10YR5/4) friable loam without distinct structure
B_2	25–50 cm.	Yellowish-brown (7.5YR5/6) fine blocky fairly stiff clay with small pieces of ferruginous very fine-grained sandstone. Friable when moist and plastic when wet
C	50 cm. +	Slabby, very fine-grained sandstone with streaks of brown iron oxide

(After Thorp)

scape. In Australia, with less rainfall, these yellow podzolic soils are frequently affected by the presence of salts, leached from upslope, and yet not transported right out of the landscape. As a result, features of a solonetzic nature can be seen in the profiles.

In the past, American pedologists thought a change in climate had occurred since these soils were originally formed, so that the present leached profile had developed from a soil which had more affinities with those in the more humid tropics. If this were so, the red and yellow pod-

8.5 Diagrammatic profile of a red-yellow podzolic soil

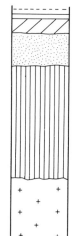

L+F	
A	Acid mineral and organic horizon
Eb	Lighter coloured acid eluvial horizon thicker in yellow soils
B	Red or brownish-red horizon rich in clay which increases with depth. Iron more hydrated in yellow soils
C	Parent material formed from wide range of geological materials

zolic soils would resemble the red and brown Mediterranean soils, which are thought by French pedologists to possess signs of leaching as well as ferrallitization. Recent American work has tended to discredit climatic change as an important factor in the formation of the red and yellow podzolic soils.

Although widely known by the name red-yellow podzolic soils, they have recently been reclassified in the U.S. Soil Taxonomy as belonging to the order Ultisols.

Many of these soils have lost iron from the eluvial horizon which becomes bleached and, where the parent material is very sandy, podzol development can take place in the upper part of the soil profile resulting in a bisequal soil. A feature which these soils have in common with many soils of the humid tropics is that some of them have subsoil material which will harden irreversibly on exposure to the atmosphere. Material such as this is called plinthite and occurs where there is a seasonally fluctuating ground-water level; usually it can be recognised by the presence of bright red mottles. In other examples induration of the subsoil occurs in the form of a fragipan, usually attributed to close-packing of mineral grains as a result of freeze-thaw action during a phase of periglacial climate. This has resulted in many different suborders including Aquults, Ustults, Xerults, Humults and Udults with Pale-, Plinthic-, Fragic- great groups being identified. Appropriate names from the F.A.O./U.N.E.S.C.O. World Soil Map Legend would include Orthic, Plinthic, Gleyic Acrisols as well as some Nitosols.

Soils of the temperate continental interiors

The *chernozems*, or *black earths*, (Mollisols; Chernozems; Phaeozems) occur on the natural grasslands of the North American prairie and Russian steppes. The formation of these soils results from a delicate balance of temperature, rainfall and vegetation brought about by their geographical location in the continental interiors. While the chestnut soils (Ustolls; Kastanozems) are developed towards the drier desert margins, prairie soils (Udolls; Phaeozems) and varieties of leached chernozem form a transition to the leached soils of cool temperate climates.

Modern approaches to soil classification require that a soil must meet the criteria of certain diagnostic horizons before it can be allocated to a category. In the case of the soils of the humid and sub-humid grasslands of the world it is primarily the possession of a mollic epipedon or a mollic A horizon. This may be combined with various sub-surface diagnostic horizons such as an argillic, calcic, natric or gypsic horizon to give the great groups of the U.S. Soil Taxonomy or the units of the Soil Map of the World. The darkening of the soil by accumulation of humus, a process referred to as melanization by some writers, involves the development of resistant ligno-protein residues which give a black colour to the soil (see p. 86).

Chernozems

In parts of Romania, Hungary and the Ukraine southeast of Kiev, as well as west-central Siberia, the main soil type is the chernozem. This soil also occurs in North America, west of longitude 95° W and north of the Arkansas River, but the area is very much smaller than that of the Eurasian chernozems. According to Russian sources, almost 2,000,000 square kilometres of their country is covered by chernozems, which is about half the world area of these soils. Chernozems, or black earths similar to them, occur in all habitable continents, but there are differences of opinion about the status of black earth soils in Africa (*vlei* soils), Australia, India (regur or black cotton soil) and South America which do not possess all the properties of the true chernozem (see Vertisols p. 86).

The chernozems (Borolls, Udolls, Ustolls, Xerolls; Chernozems, Phaeozems) have developed south of the forest-steppe ecotone on the steppes of Russia and the prairies of U.S.A. and Canada. In both the continents where they are of major occurrence, the chernozems are developed upon loess or loess-like parent materials. Outside those areas of the northern hemisphere covered by ice during the Pleistocene Glaciations, tundra climate prevailed, and as the glaciers melted much glacial debris, from moraines and outwash streams, was left without a vegetative cover. Winnowed by the wind, the fine dust from these deposits was transported and redeposited as loess. This has formed the parent material for the chernozem soils in favourable areas, though it is also found as a constituent of the parent material of soils elsewhere (Fig. 8.6).

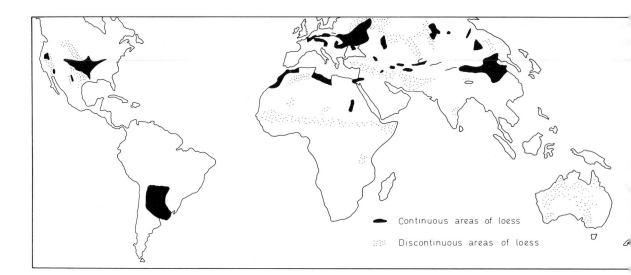

The climate of the continental interior has a cold winter with temperatures between $-7\,°C$ and $-10\,°C$, and the soil is frozen to a depth of 60–80 cm. from November to April. The winter snow cover is not deep. There is an annual precipitation of 550 mm., with a slight rainfall maximum in the summer months. Temperatures in July are in the range $19\,°C–21\,°C$. There is a period of 150 to 160 days without a killing frost during the year. Chernozem soils occur in a number of climatic divisions. According to Köppen these are humid continental with short summer (Cwa), humid continental with long summer (Dfa, Dwa), and semi-arid, middle-latitude steppe (BSk).

In the U.S. Soil Taxonomy moisture conditions are an important criteria for classification at suborder level. Udolls are continually moist in the B horizon or the soil is dry for less than 60 consecutive days in seven years out of ten. Ustolls are dry for 90 days per year, of which not more than 60 are consecutive days, and Xerolls are dry for more than 60 consecutive days each year in seven years out of ten. These three suborders include soils which have formed in mean annual temperatures of more than $8\,°C$, whereas the Borolls have formed in mean annual temperatures of less than $8\,°C$.

Chernozem soils occur naturally beneath a grassland composed of a large number of genera including *Agropyron*, *Bouteloua*, *Buchloe*, *Poa* and *Stipa*. Herbaceous plants are common, and patches of trees including oak and lime are characteristic of the ecotone of the forests to the north. This landscape, a gently undulating plain where grasses and small herbaceous plants once formed a dense ground cover, is now mainly cultivated.

The environmental factors which control the formation of these soils depend on warm spring and summer temperatures with adequate moisture supply from snow-melt and from the early summer rain. The rapid growth of grasses and herbs produces a large amount of root and aerial shoots. The drought of late summer and the frosts of winter largely arrest the process of decomposition. Consequently, losses of organic matter are minimised, and as humus formation takes place in a neutral environment rich in calcium, the mull or calcareous mull form of humus results. Chernozems have a rich fauna which incorporates the humus into the deep A horizon, and the soil is also worked through by small vertebrates, the former presence of which is shown by their infilled burrows, known as krotovinas (Fig. 8.7 and Plate 15).

The deep humus-enriched A horizon 80–100 cm. thick with its well-developed crumb-granular structure is characteristic of the 'typical chernozem'. The humus content ranges from about 10 per cent at the surface to 2 per cent at

Profile of a typical chernozem (Boroll; Calcic Chernozem) from near Kursk, U.S.S.R.
(Parent material – loess over sandstone)

	0– 5 cm.	Compact root mat of grasses
A_{11}	5– 60 cm.	Uniform dark grey clayey upper part of the humus horizon with fine crumb-granular structure; friable; roots mostly in the 0–40 cm. layer; gradual boundary
A_{12}	60–100 cm.	Dark grey, cinnamonic-tinged, clayey lower part of the humus horizon with crumb-nutty structure; more compact consistence than above; effervescence below 90 cm. gradual boundary
A/C_{ca}	100–120 cm.	Many dark grey krotovinas and worm burrows in a cinnamonic-pale yellow background; silty clay with crumb-nutty structure; abundant pseudo-mycelium; gradual boundary
C_{ca}	120–250 cm.	Light pale-yellow loamy calcareous horizon; weak prismatic structure; firm; porous; dispersed carbonate
		(After Afanasyeva)

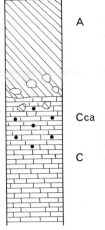

A	Mull humus incorporated to considerable depth by earthworms, neutral or slightly acid
	Krotovinas (burrows) of vertebrate animals
Cca	Parent material of loess or loess-like loams, concentration of $CaCo_3$ in Cca horizon but depth varies
C	according to amount of leaching

8.7 Diagrammatic profile of a chernozem

the lower boundary of the A horizon, and the carbon : nitrogen ratio is in the range 11–12. As the clay minerals are of the montmorillonitic variety, the exchange capacity and fertility is high. Chernozems are slightly leached, so their upper horizons are neutral or slightly acid. The passage of moisture through the profile is downwards in spring following snow-melt. During summer evaporation from the surface reverses the process so that the soil is rarely wetted to beyond a depth of 1.5 to 2.0 m. It is this mild leaching and re-evaporation which leads to the concentration of calcareous material in the lower part of the profile and which retains soil nutrients within the rooting zone.

The calcium carbonate horizon in the example given extends from 90 to 180 cm., and has a maximum content at 120–130 cm. The upper part of the accumulation is characterised by 'pseudo-mycelia', a filamentous form of carbonate concretion. In the zone of maximum accumulation carbonate concretions occupy the former pores and cavities in the loess, and even form small nodules. The typical chernozem of Russia has a maximum carbonate content in the upper part of the ca horizon, which occurs at shallow depth, even in the A horizon. Therefore, it can be distinguished from the leached chernozem where the accumulation occurs lower in the profile and the maximum carbonate content occurs in the middle of the ca horizon. These variations of leaching can be related to the micro-relief, for with the spring snow-melt, water is concentrated into the depressions of the landscape where more leaching takes place than on higher areas (Fig. 8.8).

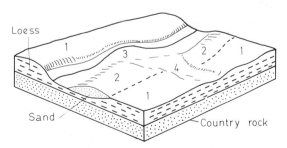

8.8 Chernozems and their relationship to the landscape
1. Typical (deep) chernozems developed on freely drained interfluve areas
2. Sandy river terraces with leached brown earth or even podzol soils
3. Soils of the alluvium
4. Leached and podzolized chernozems of the topographic depressions

In North America, the prairie soils (Udolls; Phaeozems), are roughly equivalent to these degraded (leached) chernozems. Both occur on the moister, wooded boundary of the typical chernozems. Prairie soils have a profile in which a dark, humus-rich A horizon overlies a brown, compact B horizon. This B horizon is absent from typical chernozems and represents the first sign of an illuvial horizon in the sequence of soils from chernozems to grey-brown podzolic soils. The horizon of calcium carbonate accumulation occurs below the B horizon, which effectively separates it from the organic-rich surface horizon. The prairie soils, with their leached profile typical of forested soils further north and east, with their organic-rich horizons typical of the grasslands, present problems of genesis which are as yet unsolved. Southwards, in Oklahoma and Texas where hot dry summers are experienced, the prairie soils become redder in colour and were formerly known as reddish-brown prairie soils, corresponding to Argiustolls or Luvic Phaeozems.

In regions with a drier climate the production of organic matter for the A horizon becomes less, leading Russian pedologists to recognise *ordinary* and *southern* chernozems. Ordinary chernozems

have less organic matter (5.0 per cent) and southern chernozems an even lower amount (3.50 per cent). Higher temperatures cause the oxidation of the organic matter to proceed at a greater rate, while with a lower rainfall the volume of plant material produced is less. The thickness of the A horizon decreases, and carbonate accumulation takes place nearer the surface (Plate 16).

Chestnut soils
Both American and Russian pedologists have described soils of the drier parts of the short-grass steppe and prairie as *chestnut soils* (Ustolls; Kastanozems) (Plate 17). These soils occur in the extreme south of the Ukraine, and in a broad arc from the western shore of the Caspian Sea eastwards along latitude 50° N as far as the Irtysh River. Beyond the Altai Mountains these soils are widespread in eastern Outer Mongolia and northern Manchuria. In North America, chestnut soils extend from the North Saskatchewan River south-eastwards to the Llano Estacado on the High Plains east of the Rockies.

A vegetation of 'mixed prairie' grasses is characteristic of these grasslands which are composed of the species *Stipa*, bunch grasses as well as lower, more drought-resistant grasses of the species *Bouteloua* and *Aristida*. Salt-tolerant

8.9 Soils of the chestnut and southern chernozem zone of the southern Ukraine

1. Chestnut soil or southern chernozem
2. Solonetz on slopes
3. Solod on depression floor

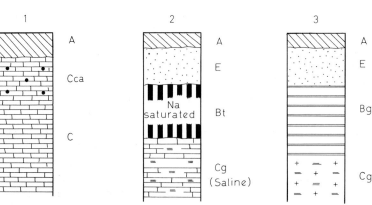

plants such as *Artemisia*, sagebrush, and even cacti are components of the vegetation in the driest parts of this soil zone. The growth of plants is limited by the low rainfall, 340 to 360 mm. per annum, and there is a high rate of evapotranspiration. Temperatures of 20 °C to 25 °C are experienced during the summer, and freezing winter temperatures are possible over much of the area where these soils occur. The supply of organic matter is much less than in the chernozem soils, and the humus is of the mull type. The A horizon is reduced in thickness to less than 25 cm., prismatic structure becomes well developed in the B horizon and the accumulation of calcium carbonate occurs between 40 cm. and 50 cm. from the surface.

The parent material of these soils in the U.S.S.R. is mostly a loess overlying older sediments, but the example given from the U.S.A. is formed from a calcareous drift.

Profile of a chestnut soil (Argiustoll; Luvic Kastanozem) from Williams County, North Dakota
(Parent material – calcareous glacial till)

A_{11}	0– 3 cm.	Brown (10YR5/2 dry) to very dark brown (10YR2/2 moist) loam with soft crumb structure, neural or mildly alkaline
A_{12}	3–10 cm.	Brown (10YR4/2 dry) to very dark brown (10YR2/2 moist) loam with weak platy structure readily crushed to a medium crumb; neutral or mildly alkaline
A_3	10–25 cm.	Brown (10YR4/2 dry) to dark brown (10YR3/2 moist) silt loam with moderate prismatic structure; neutral to slightly acid
B_2	25–50 cm.	Greyish-brown (2.5YR5/2 dry) to dark greyish-brown (2.5YR4/2 moist) heavy loam with strong prismatic structure in the upper part and very coarse blocky below; slightly calcareous
C_{ca}	50–65 cm.	Light greyish-brown (2.5YR6/2 dry) to yellowish-brown (2.5Y5/4 moist) friable massive or weak coarse subangular blocky loam or silt loam, highly calcareous.
C	65 cm.	Light grey (2.5Y7/2 dry) to yellowish-brown (2.5Y5/4 moist) sandy clay or clay loam till
		(After U.S.D.A.)

An interesting pattern of soil distribution has developed on the drier steppes of the southern Ukraine in the zone of chestnut soils. This pattern is related to the micro-relief. Broad shallow depressions occur which receive water following the spring snow-melt. Because of the movement of water through the soil into these depressions, there is a tendency for soluble salts to accumulate but, at the same time, the additional water can cause leaching of the salts to greater depth in the soils of the depressions (Fig. 8.9). A dynamic situation exists with the salts migrating down through the soil in a wetter season, and accumulating nearer the surface in a drier season. This has led to the formation of a whole range of solonetz and solodized solonetz soils where halomorphic and hydromorphic features are associated (Chapter 10).

Soils of the semi-desert and desert areas

It is estimated by Russian pedologists that 17 per cent of the earth's surface has desert soils. Their extent varies considerably from continent to continent, with Australia 44 per cent, Africa 37 per cent and Eurasia 15 per cent of their land area coming into this category. The desert regions of the world have a severe climate, in which special weathering conditions prevail and in which there is a highly specialised plant and animal life. Almost all soil classifications distinguish a group of desert soils. These occur in a broad zone across Africa and Asia where they are interrupted by the various mountain ranges, the central part of Australia and smaller areas in North and South America.

The climate of the deserts is characterised by an irregular and insufficient rainfall which does not provide enough moisture for leaching. Long periods of complete drought may be broken by brief torrential showers, while the average rainfall may be less than 150 mm. per annum. Temperatures during the day are high, but during the night there is a rapid fall in temperature, often ranging over 40 °C. Frost is common on more elevated areas of the temperate deserts. Low atmospheric humidity and few clouds combine to give uninterrupted sunshine, so that soil-surface temperatures of 43 °C are recorded. These areas are climatically classified by Köppen as middle latitude desert (Bwk) and low latitude desert (Bwh).

Desert soils fall into two main categories, those with evidence of soil formation similar to other soils and those with physical differentiations only. The former have traditionally been referred to as Sierozems and the latter as Raw Mineral Soils. Recent approaches to their classification stresses the importance of calic, gypsic or argillic horizons. They fall within the order of Aridisols in the U.S. Soil Taxonomy and in the Yermosols or Xerosols of the F.A.O./U.N.E.S.C.O. World Soil Map Legend.

Sierozems

Grey desert soils or *sierozem* (Aridisols; Xerosols) occur in areas where there is about 250 mm. or less average annual rainfall which comes in irregular showers. With a limited amount of organic matter, these soils have free calcium carbonate or gypsum at or just below the surface. They are developed beneath a vegetation described as 'desert-shrub' in the intermontane valleys of Colorado, New Mexico and Utah. The sagebrush (*Artemisia*) and bunch-grasses are the most common components of this vegetation. In Russia the grey desert soils occur in the foothill regions of the Kazakh and Tajik Republics of the U.S.S.R. where they are extensively irrigated for cotton production.

Profiles examined on loess-like terrace deposits in Tajikistan possess weak but obvious A horizons. When cultivated these soils are extremely friable with a weak crumb structure. Below the A horizon structure becomes less obvious but gypsum and calcareous concretions give lighter colours. The depth of these concretionary deposits depends considerably upon the amount and length of time irrigation has been practised. Desert and semi-desert soils occur which have a cambic B horizon (Camborthids; Haplic Xerosols) or an argillic B horizon (Haplargids; Luvic Xerosols) but many profiles are also rich in calcium carbonate or gypsum (Calciorthids; Calcic or Gypsic Xerosols).

Raw mineral soils

Mechanical weathering produces a coarse regolith, and although there is a lack of surface water in the deserts, some chemical weathering occurs

below ground. Additionally, a process called salt weathering occurs which involves the increase in volume of salt crystals leading to the granular disruption of rocks and building materials. The weathered material is redistributed by wind and sheetflood, so that the parent material for soil formation is often well differentiated into rocky areas, dune areas with sandy textures and playa floors with silt or clay textures (Plate 18). The name *raw mineral soils* (Aridisols; Yermosols) is used to describe materials in which soil horizon development is minimal. Salts tend to accumulate when waters evaporate from the lower-lying areas (Fig. 8.10). Although the presence of salts is wide-

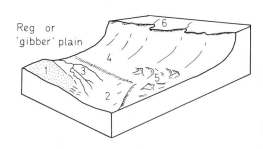

8.10 Block diagram to show the relationship of desert soils to the landscape
1. Reg or stony desert
2. Clay pan (saline)
3. Alluvial tract
4. Red or grey desert soils
5. Erg or dune sand
6. Plateau formed by duricrust

spread in arid areas, they do not occur in all desert soils; usually it is a shortage of water rather than the presence of salts which is the limiting factor for plant life. Plant nutrients may be available in suitable forms, but the lack of water restricts their uptake and the growth of plants is inhibited.

Even though there is insufficient moisture for regular downward leaching, there are movement of soil constituents in desert soils. Some movement occurs in an upward direction as is shown by the crusts of calcium carbonate and calcium sulphate, as well as the *desert lac* of iron oxides

Whilst some of these may be contemporary features, others have been formed in a previously moister climate of a Pleistocene pluvial period and are thus relic features. Illuvial accumulations can be revealed at the surface by the winnowing away of the overlying soil material.

Plant growth is sparse and organic matter supplies are low because of the rigorous climate. Strong oxidising conditions at the surface, and wind which removes dead vegetation, severely limit the amount of humus which is incorporated into the soil. Average figures can be misleading, but those quoted range from less than $\frac{1}{2}$ per cent to 2 per cent of organic matter in desert soils. The lack of available moisture in the desert is reflected in the plant distributions which closely reflect the drainage and soil patterns. The different soils have their effect on plant distributions according to their ability to supply water to plants.

Material best described as desert detritus can be found in the sand deserts (*ergs*), the clay plains and desert pavements (*regs*). Normal profile development is absent and there is little biological activity.

Weakly developed soils (Entisols, Aridisols; Fluvisols, Regosols, Yermosols) are fairly common in Africa and an example is given from South Africa. These youthful soils lack well-developed horizons because of limited organic matter, leaching, erosion, or accretion.

Profile of a desert soil (Calciorthid; Calcic Yermosol) from near the Sak river, South Africa (Parent material — schists)

Surface	Angular shale fragments and stones cover the surface (desert pavement), but desert pigment is not conspicuous
0–15 cm.	Light yellowish-brown sandy clay loam; vesicular, and easily crushed to powder; roots few and thin; organic matter absent
15–45 cm.	Light reddish-brown with whitish tint, coarse sandy clay loam; fairly dense; occasional calcium carbonate concretion
45 cm. +	Platy undecomposed schist

(After C. R. Van der Merwe)

Development of desert pavement is ascribed to two processes. The removal by wind of finer material from the surface leaves the stones to form a protective covering. Immediately below the surface layer of stones the mineral soil is characterised by a porous, vesicular structure which has formed, it is thought, by the action of repeated wetting and drying cycles during which the stones move upwards leaving a relatively stone-free layer with pores formed when air is entrapped below the stone. This is essentially raw mineral material rather than true soil. In Africa alone, 'non-soils' such as these occupy 28 per cent of the entire continent.

9 SOILS OF THE LOW LATITUDES

The discussion of the factors of soil formation in Chapter 3 has already shown that there is a theoretical possibility of the most rapid weathering in the humid tropical regions of the world. The breakdown of the rocks and formation of the regolith has proceeded more rapidly, and has had no interruption in contrast with the temperate regions where Pleistocene Glaciations drastically changed the climate in relatively recent times. Consequently, there is on average a greater depth of regolith in the tropical regions, with more than 30 m. recorded at some places. In the past there has been great confusion as to the definition of a soil in the tropics, confusion which has obscured present ideas of soil formation. If the soil is thought of as that part of the earth's crust influenced by current soil formation and exploited by plant roots, this does avoid the confusion between soil and parent material. However, in tropical regions as elsewhere, it is necessary to understand conditions in the parent material as these may influence processes in the soil itself.

Many inter-tropical areas have been dry land for long periods of geological history, and the deposits upon them are deeply weathered terrestrial materials dating back to the Miocene or Pliocene. Geomorphologists have recognised several surfaces associated with cycles of erosion of different ages. These surfaces have soils of different ages upon them with different profiles and properties. Some redistribution has taken place of the deposits of these surfaces resulting in a complicated pattern of soils, which can be understood only if their mode of origin is first deciphered. Concepts of erosional and depositional phases of soils, developed in Australia, have greatly assisted the elucidation of the soil pattern found on these old continental blocks (Fig. 9.1).

Humid tropical regions are characterised by a continually moist environment with a pattern of two precipitation maxima, a total rainfall of 2000 mm. or more, and a mean annual temperature of 25 °C with only slight daily variation. This continually hot, humid climate is classed as humid tropical, continually wet (Af) by Köppen. Towards the tropics, a dry season occurs and there is

9.1 Erosional and depositional phases of soils
(after B. E. Butler)

Zone beyond deposition unaffected

Zone of soil deposition

Zone of soil erosion

Zone beyond erosion unaffected

Erosion in time 1 only

Erosion in time 2 and 1

Accretion in time 1 only

Accretion in time 2 and 1

Original surface

Original surface

1a   First erosional surface
1b   First depositional surface
2a   Second erosional surface
2b   Second depositional surface

only one rainy season corresponding with the overhead sun. Rainfall varies considerably with location from 600 mm. to 1500 mm. per annum, and although the average temperatures are similar to those of the humid regions, the range (20 °C) is much greater. These are called savanna climates (Aw).

The climatic changes associated with the Pleistocene also affected the margins of the tropical areas. It is known from biogeographical evidence that the Sahara has been considerably moister than at present, and also that the present savanna has been subjected to a drier climate. During these dry phases restricted vegetative growth led to more rapid natural soil erosion. In the moist or pluvial phases, the vegetative balance was changed with more trees growing and greater soil stability.

The dense tropical rain forest of the humid tropical regions provides a continual supply of plant nutrients from the litter. If the cycle of nutrients from plant to soil and back to plant is broken by clearing the forest, a rapid decline in fertility is noted. Away from the continually humid regions, deciduous tress which shed their leaves in the dry season become more common, and eventually these give way to the savanna grasslands. Fire is a much greater danger in these regions as once the grasses are burnt the soil has no protective cover and is easily eroded.

The soils of the humid tropical regions are leached, producing a neutral to moderately acid pH value but, because of the bases supplied from the litter, strongly acid conditions do not develop. In these conditions, silica is more soluble than iron oxides and is lost from the structure of the clay minerals. The iron and aluminium oxides which remain are relatively insoluble. Where these form an obvious part of a soil horizon it is an *oxic* horizon. The presence of the iron sesquioxides gives the soils a red coloration which is characteristic of most freely drained tropical soils (Plate 19). The greater solubility of silica from the clay minerals is demonstrated by the composition of drainage waters of tropical rivers. Examples are recorded where amounts of up to 50 per cent of total solids carried by rivers in the tropics consist of silica whereas the average content of all rivers only amounts to 12 per cent. However, recent studies of weathering indicate that silica is lost in

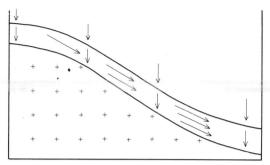

9.2 Schematic diagram of the movements of soil constituents including water, clay sesquioxides and organic colloids on a slope. Compare with the diagram of a catena (Fig. 11.2)

the first stage of rock weathering, while that which remains as quartz or kaolinite is relatively stable.

The greater mobility of soil constituents in tropical soils is seen also in the soil pattern and its relationship to the landscape. Movement downslope of soil constituents brings into being a sequence of soils, related to relief, known as a catena (Figs. 9.2 and 11.2). Soil development in the tropical regions does not take place in a vertical direction only as is often assumed in considerations of the soils of temperate regions.

In freely drained conditions, the possibility of illuvial deposition in a B horizon is rather unlikely as the chemical environment of the deep regolith is similar throughout. In soils which have formed in a climate with a well-marked dry season, it is possible that silica may be deposited lower in the regolith. The precipitation of silica is a fairly common feature of semi-desert areas of Australia where a silica-enriched horizon occurs, known as *silcrete*, which erosion may subsequently reveal at the surface as a *duricrust*.

The character of the iron oxides remaining in the soil depends largely upon the water relationships of the soil. With freely drained soils of interfluve areas, the iron oxides remain dispersed throughout the profile, but if ground-water is in close proximity to the surface, then the development of a grey soil with red mottles which hardens on exposure to air occurs. This is called plinthite in the U.S. Soil Taxonomy. Where a large amount of concretionary iron has accumulated and subsequently hardened, it has a rock-like pisolitic, nodular or slag-like appearance, and is known as laterite (p. 89).

Table 9.1   *Synonyms for soils of low latitudes*

Common Names	U.S. Soil Taxonomy	F.A.O./ U.N.E.S.C.O. World Map Legend
Ferrallitic soils Red-yellow latosols Dark red latosols Brown latosols Ferrallitic soils Ferrisols (in part) Kaolisols	Oxisols	Ferralsols
Ferruginous soils Red-yellow podzolic soils (in part) Krasnozems Ferrisols (in part) Ferruginous soils Zheltozems	Ultisols	Acrisols Nitosols
Podzols Vertisols Acid sulphate soils Paddy soils Laterite	Spodosols Vertisols	Podzols Vertisols

There have been numerous approaches to the study and classification of soils in low latitudes. The early Russian pioneers observed the development of red 'zonal' soils in tropical regions and in recent years Soviet pedologists have identified red

9.3 Diagrammatic profiles of ferrallitic and ferruginous soils

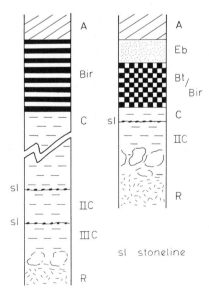

sl stoneline

earths (krasnozems) and yellow earths (zheltozems). The use of the term laterite and its derivative latosol bedevilled soil nomenclature elsewhere in the world for many years and this word is now restricted in its use to features which result from iron and aluminium segregation (see p. 89). In classifications developed by French pedologists the soils of the humid tropical regions are the Ferrallitic soils and the Ferruginous soils are those of the savanna lands with strongly alternating wet and dry seasons. The Ferrallitic soils do not have evidence of clay migration into the B horizon, and the development of an argillic horizon is usually a characteristic feature of the Ferruginous soils. Therefore, it is easy to see how the present approach to classification of the soils of the inter-tropical regions of the world was developed. There are two main groups of soils: Ferrallitic soils with oxic B horizons (Oxisols; Ferralsols) and Ferruginous soils with argillic B horizons (Ultisols; Acrisols, Nitosols) (Fig. 9.3). Local variations in elevation and parent material such as coarse siliceous deposits, volcanic ashes, limestone, marine and fresh water alluvia all produce soils of different character which do not fit the broad zonal pattern of soils identified by late nineteenth and early twentieth century pedologists.

Ferrallitic soils (Oxisols; Ferralsols)
The ferrallitic soils include those soils previously referred to as ferrallitic soils, latosols or kaolisols as shown in Table 9.1. They are very old, deep and highly weathered soils of the humid tropics formed at elevations of less than 2000 m. Ferrallitic soils are those which satisfy the criteria for an oxic B horizon. In a horizon at least 30 cm thick, they possess a low cation exchange capacity with no more than traces of primary minerals remaining following prolonged exposure to soil forming processes. The oxic horizon consists of a mixture of hydrated oxides of iron and aluminium with variable amounts of kaolinitic clays and quartz sand. There is no illuvial accumulation of clay and there is little clay which is dispersable in water because it is cemented by iron oxides.

A soil map of Africa which has been widely accepted distinguishes four main groups of soils characteristic of the humid and sub-humid tropics. These are ferrallitic soils, ferrisols, ferrugi

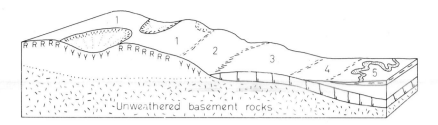

9.4 Soils of the humid tropical regions
1. Red leached ferrallitic soils (R)
2. Yellow leached ferrallitic soils (Y)
3. Vertisols on calcareous parent material
4. Gley soils
5. Alluvial soils

Profile of an Orthic Ferralsol (Orthox; Ferralsol)
from Rio Clara, Brazil
(Parent material – shales)

A 0– 30 cm. Dark reddish brown (2.5YR3/4) clay with strong medium granular structure; very plastic and very sticky; abundant roots; gradual smooth boundary

A/B 30– 60 cm. Dark red (2.5YR3/6) clay with weak compound prismatic structure breaking to moderate medium sub-angular blocky; plastic and sticky; abundant roots; gradual boundary

B$_1$ 60–150 cm. Dark red (2.5YR3/6) clay with weak compound prismatic structure breaking easily to fine and very fine granular; slightly plastic and slightly sticky; few roots; diffuse smooth boundary

B$_2$ 150–210 cm. Dark red (10YR3/6) with common prominent dark grey (5YR4/1) mottles, clay with massive structure which breaks easily to weak sub-angular blocky and fine granular structure; slightly plastic and slightly sticky; abrupt boundary

BC 210–260 cm. Dark red (10YR3/6) with common prominent dark grey (5YR4/1) mottles, clay with massive structure which breaks to weak medium subangular blocky and fine granular structure; slightly plastic and sticky; abrupt boundary

C 260–280 cm. White (2.5YR8/0) and dark grey (5YR4/1) clay
        (After Bennema)

nous soils and vertisols. The first three are freely drained red soils, and the Vertisols by contrast are dark in colour and seasonally poorly drained. In the legend for the F.A.O./U.N.E.S.C.O. World Soil Map the concept of the Ferralsols includes ferrallitic soils, ferrisols and part of the ferruginous tropical soils. In this account, attention is drawn to two basic types of ferrallitic soils: the leached ferrallitic soils of the humid tropics and the weathered ferrallitic soils of the savanna lands.

In the humid rain forest regions strongly leached soils have developed which correspond to the Ferrallitic soils (Acrorthox, Acric Ferralsols), (Fig. 9.4). These soils represent the most intensive stage of weathering and leaching as they have little or no reserve of weatherable minerals. The clay minerals are of the kaolinite type with a low cation exchange capacity. Horizon differentiation is weak and the deep profile is characterised by a porous consistence and a granular to sub-angular blocky structure. These are soils with low fertility and low agricultural value. The profile of an Orthic Ferralsol described from Brazil illustrates this important soil grouping.

Similarly strongly weathered soils occur in the savanna lands having a low exchange capacity but lacking the strong leaching and acidity of the soils of the humid rainforest. In previous work these soils have been described as 'plateau soils' or 'pallid soils' as they occur on gently undulating plateau surfaces in savanna lands. These soils, it has been suggested, should be distinguished as *weathered ferrallitic soils* (Eutrorthox; Orthic Ferralsol). Both leached and weathered ferrallitic soils together with the similar Ferrisols are considered to be Ferralsols in the F.A.O./U.N.E.S.C.O. World Soil Map Legend and correspond broadly to the Orthox and Humox suborders of the U.S. Soil Taxonomy.

Ferruginous soils (Ultisols; Acrisols, Nitosols)

Many tropical soils possess an argillic B horizon, often with an extended distribution in depth. The strong leaching experienced in humid tropical environments has brought the base saturation to below 50 per cent saturation and the colours throughout are brown or reddish brown. In spite of the strong leaching, these soils do not develop the bleached horizon characteristic of the comparable red-yellow podzolic soils of the southeast U.S.A. Two main types of ferruginous soils are recognised in the F.A.O./U.N.E.S.C.O. Soil Map Legend. Acrisols have a clear-cut argillic B horizon, the clay content of which decreases below the B horizon whereas in the Nitosols the increased content of clay is maintained to much greater depth.

The Acrisols and Nitosols include soils previously known as red-yellow podzolic soils, some ferruginous tropical soils, ferrisols, kraznozems and zheltozems. Acrisols and Nitosols can be dealt with together in an account such as this which attempts to review the soils of the world. In both groups leaching has resulted in very acid clayey soils in which an illuvial accumulation of clay has occurred under conditions of low base saturation. In colour, these soils usually are browner or yellower than the Ferrallitic soils and the gleyic Acrisols are grey. The fine texture results in an angular blocky structure but prismatic structures are rarely developed according to descriptions available. Poorly drained subgroups are identified as Gleyic or Plinthic Acrisols, but no poorly drained soils have been recognised in the Nitosols.

9.5 Soils of the savanna lands
1. Weathered ferrallitic soils (Ferralsols)
2. Laterite, indurated at plateau edge forming a 'breakaway'
3. Ferruginous soils (Acrisols)
4. Vertisols
5. Alluvial soils

Profile of a Dystric Nitosol (Udult; Nitosol) from Nicaragua
(Parent material − basic volcanic tuff or basalt)

Ah	0− 15 cm.	Dark reddish brown (5YR3/3) clay loam with fine angular blocky structure; friable, slightly plastic, slightly sticky; gradual boundary
Bt$_1$	16− 60 cm.	Dark reddish brown (5YR3/3) clay with strong coarse angular blocky structure, breaking easily to medium and fine angular blocky; plastic and slightly sticky
Bt$_2$	60−120 cm.	Distinctly mottled dark red and reddish brown (5YR4/3) clay with strong coarse angular blocky breaking easily to medium angular blocky structure; plastic, slightly sticky; strong clay-skins on ped faces
BC	120−200 cm.	Prominently mottled dark red (2.5YR3/6) and reddish grey (5YR5/2) clay; strong clay-skins on coarse angular blocky structure

(After Smyth)

Ferruginous soils were originally described from areas where there is a pronounced dry season, for example in Africa where they occupy 11 per cent of the surface of the continent. These soils are found on acid crystalline basement rocks beneath dry woodland and savanna in northern Nigeria and Ghana (Fig. 9.5). Horizon development is better than in the ferrallitic soils and as a result of leaching of clay and iron compounds, an eluvial horizon can be seen, below which a textural B horizon is developed. There are often some

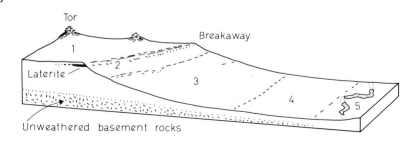

reserves of weatherable minerals present. Although the clays are kaolinitic, the exchange capacity is higher than in ferrallitic soils particularly in the B horizon. These soils are seldom deep, and fresh rock is frequently found between 100 and 250 cm. below the surface. The example below is from central Ghana. The stone lines indicate that the soil is polygenetic with different layers of parent material suggesting that this soil has been re-worked from pre-existing materials (Fig. 9.3).

Profile of an Acrisol (Ustult; Acrisol) from Ejura, Ghana
(Parent material – sandstone)

Ap	0– 28 cm.	Dark reddish brown (2.5YR2/4), becoming dark red (2.5YT3/6) with depth, loamy sand with very weak fine granular structure; many fine roots; clear wavy boundary
E/B	28– 75 cm.	Red (2.5YR4/6) sandy clay loam becoming dark red (10R3/6) sandy clay with weak fine subangular blocky structure; few fine roots; clear smooth boundary
Bt	75–155 cm.	Red (10YR4/6) clay with massive structure but friable when disturbed; few fine roots; thin stone line; abrupt smooth boundary
IIB	115–182 cm.	Red (10YR4/6) gravelly clay with massive structure with up to 35 per cent ironstone gravel and pieces of ferruginised rock and a stone line; abrupt wavy boundary
IIC	182–258 cm.	Red (10YR4/6) sandy clay loam with massive structure containing weathering sandstone (After Adu and Tenadu)

The name *krasnozem* was given to tropical and sub-tropical red soils developed upon base-rich parent materials. The name was first used in the Trans-Caucasian regions of the U.S.S.R., and has since been used for soils in Australia, where they are developed upon basalt parent materials in Queensland and northern New South Wales (Plate 23). Originally developed under tropical rainforest, such freely drained soils lack horizon development because of the flocculating effect of their high content of hydrated ferric oxides.

Profile of a krasnozem (Udult; Nitosol) from Springbrook, Queensland
(Parent material – basalt)

	0– 25 cm.	Dark reddish-brown (5YR3/3) light clay with granular to fine blocky structure
	25–135 cm.	Red (2.5YR3/6) medium to heavy clay with blocky structure
	135–220 cm.	Brownish-red passing into reddish-brown (5YR4/4) heavy clay with blocky structure
	220–250 cm.	Reddish-brown with brownish-yellow and light grey heavy clay with blocky structure
	250–275 cm.	Yellowish-brown, light red, etc. clay loam with lumps of brittle weathered basalt

(After C.S.I.R.O.)

Krasnozems are fertile soils used for sugar-cane and pineapple in Queensland as well as for other fruit and vegetable crops. In terms of present day classification systems the word krasnozem is now no longer used and such soils would be Ultisols or Nitosols.

Profile of a yellow latosol (Udult; Ferralsol) from Cooray, Queensland
(Parent material – Permian phyllites)

	0– 6 cm.	Brown (10YR5/3) clay loam with yellowish patches; strong crumb structure
	6– 15 cm.	Brownish-yellow (10YR6/5) clay loam to light clay; fine, sub-angular, blocky structure
	15– 30 cm.	Brownish-yellow (10YR6/6) light clay with moderate blocky structure
	30– 40 cm.	Brownish-yellow with few reddish mottles, light medium clay with moderate block structure
	40– 75 cm.	Mottled brownish-red (2.5YR4/6) and brownish-yellow medium clay with strong blocky structure
	75–155 cm.	Mottled red, yellow and light grey medium clay
	155 cm. +	Weathered phyllite

(After C.S.I.R.O.)

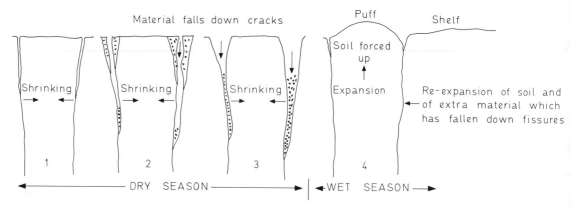

9.6 Gilgai phenomena in vertisols. Shrinkage during the dry season allows material to fall down the fissures. Expansion when wetted in the wet season results in the soil being forced up to form a ridge (puff) whilst the area around the fissures remains at a lower level (shelf)

All of these soils of the humid tropics described so far occupy positions of free drainage in the upper parts of the landscape. In lower slope positions, associated soils with more yellow colours occur where moister conditions prevail for longer periods. These soils have previously been called *yellow latosols* or *Zheltozems* (Plate 20), and are now called Orthox; Udult or Ferralsols.

Intrazonal and azonal soils are present in low latitudes and reference will be made to them in Chapter 10. In the humid tropics, the lower parts of the landscape have gley and alluvial soils. In many cases these soils have been utilised for rice cultivation and the natural soil forming processes have been strongly modified by man. These important soils are discussed separately as paddy soils (p. 87).

Podzols

Podzolization can be seen in the tropics. In Malaya, Guyana and the Congo deep 'giant' podzols have developed in alluvial sands on river terrace sites, where free drainage enables profile development to occur. An impoverished form of tropical rainforest, the 'heath forest' occurs upon these soils which are very much more deeply leached than similar temperate soils. Problems occur in the international systems of classification as the illuvial horizons are often so deep and occur below the normal soil profile depth. They have been called Quartzipsamment or Arenosols in lowland situations but more conventional podzol profiles can be found at higher altitudes in

the mountain areas of tropical lands.

Profile of a 'giant podzol' (Quartzipsamment Arenosol) from Mackenzie, Guyana
(Parent material – Berbice formation, white sand)

0– 40 cm.	Spoil
40– 55 cm.	Very dark grey (5YR3/1) sandy clay
55– 70 cm.	Very dark grey (5YR3/1) sand
70–125 cm.	Bleached white sand
125–140 cm.	Transitional to humic horizon
140–165 cm.	Black humic sand
165–180 cm.	Transitional loamy sand, very hard moist
180–200 cm.	Gleyed sandy loam resting upon iron pan 1 cm. thick
200–231 cm.	Light red (2.5YR6/5) sandy loam

(After Bleackley and Khan

Vertisols

Dark brown or black clay soils developed upon parent materials rich in bases form a special group of soils called vertisols. In areas subject to a strongly alternating climatic regime of wet and dry seasons, these soils are extensively developed. Formerly they were referred to as tropical black clays, vlei soils or black cotton soils. The U.S. Soil Taxonomy, the F.A.O./U.N.E.S.C.O. World Soil Map Legend and the French classification system all use the name vertisol, a term which has been widely accepted.

When dry, these soils shrink and crack widely so that topsoil material can fall down the cracks. After the passage of time, these soils *invert* themselves by this process. As the soil is wetted in the following wet season, the clays swell and because there is extra material in the lower horizons pressures are exerted upwards to give a micro-relief on the soil surface. This process has been described from Australia, where the phenomenon was called *gilgai* (Fig. 9.6 and Plate 22). The strong shrinkage and associated cracking is a property of montmorillonitic and mixed layer clays from which these soils are formed.

Profile of a vertisol (Vertisol; Vertisol) from Dakar, Senegal
(Parent material – marl)

0– 10 cm.	Brown-black clay, enriched with organic matter; coarse sub-angular blocky structure with glossy ped surfaces. Stable, rather porous; soil fauna very active
10– 50 cm.	Black clay with well-marked platy structure; not porous; not calcareous
50–100 cm.	Black clay, few diffuse mottles; angular blocky and platy structure, more massive, non-calcareous
100–200 cm.	Brown-black clay, small ferruginous streaks, well-developed platy structure. Numerous small calcareous nodules
200 cm. +	Marl

(After Maignien)

Dark brown vertisols occur on base-rich marls, limestones and rocks rich in ferromagnesian minerals in the sub-humid tropics, as for example, on the coastal plain of Ghana. In semi-arid areas towards the northern margin of the savanna lands, similar but black vertisols develop on alluvial lands along the major river valleys. In the former, montmorillonite clays have developed from the rich supply of elements weathering from the rocks and in the latter situation there has been an influx of elements by fluvial and colluvial action. Both dark brown and black vertisols are fertile soils which offer some of the best prospects in Africa for future agricultural development. Most vertisols described from India and Sudan are calcareous and do not have signs of poor drainage. Investigations from Trinidad have drawn attention to re-deposited montmorillonitic clays with gleyed and acid vertisols which suggests the present simple colour criteria alone are inadequate for the classification of these soils.

Acid Sulphate Soils

Soils formed from both river and estuarine alluvium are extremely important soils for paddy rice cultivation in the humid tropics, but in some cases development is restricted by the presence of acid sulphate soils. Because of continued saturation during formation these soils are strongly gleyed, and iron sulphides may occur as concretionary forms. The following profile is typical of a mangrove swamp soil.

Profile of a soil on mangrove swamp (Sulfaquent; Thionic Fluvisol), Belo, Madagascar
(Parent material – fluvio-marine alluvium)

0– 60 cm.	Yellowish-brown, clayey, plastic and adherent, rich in roots and rhizophores
60–100 cm.	Progressive transition to a greyish-blue horizon with sulphur yellow or rusty-orange mottles and cavities more or less hardened (iron sulphides), fine sandy clay, plastic
100 cm. +	Pale grey, fine sandy, rich in mica and dark minerals

(After Hervieu)

The presence of iron sulphides results from the reduction by micro-organisms of sulphur and sulphates derived from sea water. As organic matter is present also, the reduction is encouraged and the pale yellow mineral jarosite is formed. If embankment and drainage take place, aeration occurs resulting in the oxidation of ferrous sulphides to form sulphuric acid. As the soils ripen the presence of free sulphuric acid produces extremely acid conditions with pH values of between 2 and 3. Where the sediment is calcareous, acidification is less and gypsum forms instead. Acid sulphate soils or 'cat clays' have resulted from ill-advised reclamation schemes in the mangrove swamps of Surinam, Guyana, Sierra Leone and South-east Asia.

9.7 Paddy fields in Sri Lanka

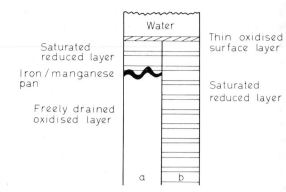

9.8 Diagrammatic profile of paddy soils (a) freely drained at depth; (b) in ground-water gley conditions

Paddy soils

An extremely important group of soils in low latitude regions are man-made soils utilised for rice growing. Although some 'upland' rice is grown, the greater part of the 125 million hectares devoted to rice cultivation takes place on soils which are flooded during the growing season. The term paddy soils includes flooded alluvial soils as well as irrigated terraces on hillsides. A wide range of soils, including most of those considered earlier in this chapter, are used for rice production throughout the tropical world (Fig. 9.7).

Characteristics which develop in paddy soils generally are associated with hydromorphism and compaction resulting from cultivation. The appearance of these soils may change greatly during the dry season when the soil is allowed to dry out. Paddy soils are usually characterised by a mottled zone with warmish, yellowish or black concretions of iron or manganese compounds. In the profile of alluvial soils (Aquents, Aquox; Fluvisols) below the mottled zone, the soil may be saturated, having permanent reducing conditions. In contrast, on terraces devoted to rice cultivation, the subsoil may be freely drained with oxidising conditions (Fig. 9.8).

Wet cultivation results in a massively struc-

Profile of an alluvial paddy soil (Aquent; Fluvisol) from Japan

(Parent material – alluvium derived from volcanic deposits and tertiary sediments)

Apg	0– 15 cm.	Dark brown (7.5YR4/2) silty clay loam with many yellowish brown and few brown mottles; clear smooth boundary
ABg	15– 24 cm.	Olive grey (5Y5/2) silty clay loam with few reddish brown and dark brown mottles; upper part (15–18 cm.) is more compact, plough-pan; clear smooth boundary
$B_{21}g$	24– 50 cm.	Light brownish grey (2.5Y6/2) silty clay, many fine, brown mottles; gradual smooth boundary
$B_{22}g$	50– 80 cm.	Olive grey (5Y5/2) silty clay, with coarse angular blocky structure and vertical fissures; common brown (10YR3/4) mottles; gradual smooth boundary
B_3g	80–100 cm.	Bluish grey (10BG5/2) silty clay common fine brown mottles; gradual wavy boundary
Cg	100 cm. +	Bluish grey (10BG5/2) silty clay, few brown mottles in upper part, unmottled below 105 cm., very sticky, very plastic

(After Kanno)

88

tured compact plough-pan below which iron and manganese compounds are often found to accumulate. This plough-pan may be emphasised by deposition of clay and silt derived from irrigation waters and from weathering *in situ*. Preparation of wet soil for planting promotes the breakdown of normal soil structure but algal growth on the surface and desiccation in the dry season tends to produce a platy structure often with bubble-shaped voids produced by gasses developed under anaerobic conditions. As an example of these soils, a profile is given from the Japanese Island of Kyushu.

Peats

High temperatures, with rapid rates of organic decomposition, limit the formation and extent of organic soils in tropical lowland areas. However, organic soils are reported from the lowlands of Sumatra and Borneo. The peat has formed from the debris of trees, unlike the moss peat of temperate climates.

Laterite (Ironstone)

So far, this discussion of the soils of the humid tropics has avoided as far as possible the use of the term laterite. *Laterite* is a phenomenon widespread in tropical areas, and is formed by an accu-

mulation in the soil of sesquioxidic material. In most cases the appearance of laterite crusts is a relic feature of a previous episode of soil formation. A *laterite horizon* is formed where the ground-water movements within the soil concentrate iron and aluminium oxides into a restricted layer (Fig. 9.9). These concentrations may appear as nodules (Plate 24), as a cellular mass or as a slag-like accumulation (Plate 25).

Profile of a laterite from near York, Western Australia
(Parent material — gneiss)

0–150 cm.	Ironstone crust	Yellowish-brown hard ironstone, becoming slightly softer towards the base
150–690 cm.	pallid zone	White and slightly pinkish clay with dark red patches. Quartz grains are bleached white in the clay and stained with iron oxide in the red. Occasional mica flakes throughout
690 cm. +	transition to parent rock	Pale brown and rusty mottled, weathered gneiss

(After Mulcahy)

In all cases where an indurated crust occurs, it seems to have suffered drying and irreversible hardening. The correct usage of the term laterite is for 'a massive vesicular or concretionary ironstone formation nearly always associated with uplifted peneplains originally associated with areas of low relief and high ground-water'. Uplift of the land surface has resulted in increased fluvial erosion by streams which have cut deeper valleys and lowered the water-table. Where it has been revealed by erosion the ironstone horizon has become irreversibly hardened by contact with the air (Plate 26). Erosion has also stripped off the overlying leached horizons so that the laterite usually occurs as a plateau remnant in an interfluve position. Good examples of this occur in Western Australia where the relic soils form part of an eroded Pliocene or Miocene surface (Plate 27). The breaking up of the laterite has formed new parent materials for soils in the present phase of soil formation. Even on the crust

9.9 Formation of laterite

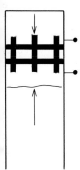

Leaching down to water-table

Concentration of iron and alluminium in nodules or slag-like concretions

Water-table steadily rising causing migration of iron and aluminium into zone alternately wet and dry

Erosion removes soil down to concretionary zone which irreversibly hardens to form crust

itself, some weathering has taken place to form a new thin soil in which a poor scrub vegetation grows. Below the crust are the mottled and pallid zones. The mottled zone is subject to some alternation of conditions, whereas the pallid zone has been completely saturated and contains only quartz sand and kaolin clay, the iron having been moved in a reduced state into the zone of the present indurated crust.

Sub-soil materials such as these which irreversibly harden on prolonged exposure to air whether sesquioxide-rich or not, are called *plinthite* in the U.S. Soil Taxonomy. This is a highly weathered mixture of clay and quartz, poor in humus and usually sesquioxide-rich, which has been subject seasonally to saturated conditions.

Laterite (plinthite) remains soft while moist and in a fresh state can be cut into blocks and then dried in the sun. Once dried and hardened it can be used as building material, for example the Angkor Wat temples in Cambodia. If a soil is stripped of its forest cover and exposed to the strong rays of the sun, it is argued that an irreversible hardening takes place, and that the areas of laterite are being extended by agricultural activities in the tropics. Where there are thin crusts, the crust can be broken and planted with trees, but whatever crop is considered, the nutrient supply of these soils is low.

10 INTRAZONAL AND AZONAL SOILS

The zonal soils considered in the previous chapters have their development influenced by the factors of soil formation with climate exerting slightly more influence than the others, producing a pattern which is roughly comparable with the climatic zones. Within the various zones are areas of well-developed soils which reflect the local dominance of a single factor such as parent material or drainage conditions. When a particular type of parent material exerts a strong influence over soil formation, as in the case of limestones, soils with *calcimorphic* characteristics are developed. In a similar manner, the continued presence of water in the soil causes the development of the features of gleying associated with *hydromorphic* soils. The presence of soluble salts in the soil confers upon it chemical, physical and biological features which require a special consideration in any classification. These are the *halomorphic* soils. These three groups of soils, calcimorphic, hydromorphic and halomorphic, form the main divisions of the intrazonal order of soils. Already they have been mentioned in the consideration of the associated zonal soils, but for completeness they are considered together in this chapter.

The identity of the intrazonal soils becomes lost in the U.S. Soil Taxonomy because they are spread throughout the subdivisions at great group level and in the World Soil Map form subdivisions of the units which comprise the legend. The presence or absence of diagnostic horizons, including calcic, gypsic, gleyic and natric horizons is critical for the allocation of these soils to their correct position in the classification.

Calcimorphic soils

The stability conferred upon a soil as the result of the presence of calcium has already been commented upon (p. 19). This property, together with the slightly alkaline pH values, results in a particular profile form and justifies the classification of calcimorphic soils as intrazonal. The profile of a soil on a limestone, compared with an adjacent soil on a non-calcareous parent material, is usually less leached and lacks strong horizon differentiation.

The mere presence of calcareous material in the soil profile is not a diagnostic feature but a calcic horizon with an amount in excess of 15 per cent calcium carbonate and 5 per cent more than the parent material is recognised. Calcic or petrocalcic horizons, the latter a continuous indurated calcic horizon, are significant in the classification of some Mollisols and Aridisols. In the World Soil Map Legend a diagnostic calcic horizon with the same criteria is used for allocation of soils to the calcic units of many different soils including Fluvisols, Cambisols, Chernozems and Yermosols.

Several features of calcareous soils make them distinct from brown earths with which they can be linked in a maturity sequence. In the first place, the vegetation growing upon these soils is usually a form which produces a leaf-litter which is rich in bases. Thus, there is a continual return of bases to the surface of the soil. Secondly, the faunal population of these soils is numerous, encouraged by the more nutritious leaf-litter. Thirdly, the presence of calcium-saturated clays and free calcium carbonate in the soil inhibits the movement of soil constituents by the formation of stable calcium compounds which remain flocculated. Fourthly, because of their stability, these soils are usually fairly rich in organic matter, have black or dark reddish-brown colours and stable structural aggregates in the form of crumb or blocky peds. Lastly, because they are formed upon rocks which have little insoluble residue, these soils are usually shallow and have low moisture reserves. As they occur over limestone, calcareous soils are invariably freely drained; however, on calcareous boulder clays transitional soils to hydromorphic soils occur, called calcareous gley soils. The two main types of profile seen are the *rendzina* (Rendoll; Rendzina) and the *brown calcareous soil* (Eutrochrept; Calcic Cambisol) (Fig. 10.1). The name rendzina, which is derived from a Polish peasant name, is widely used. Soils of this nature are described from almost all parts of the world from the temperate regions to the humid tropics. Brown calcareous soils are described from Britain and Europe, where there is some overlap with the name brown forest soils.

The rendzina is a shallow soil rich in organic matter and biological activity. It has a stable crumb structure and is dark in colour. It is a relatively simple soil with an A horizon directly overlying a C horizon which is the limestone parent material. The humus is well incorporated in the mull form, and the micro-morphological evidence shows that these soils are largely composed of the faecal pellets of soil anthropods and the casts of earthworms (Plate 28).

Profile of a rendzina (Typic Rendoll; Rendzina) from the Hartz foothills, Germany
(Parent material – chalk)

A 0–25 cm. Brownish-black, strongly humose, calcareous stony clay loam with crumb structure

C 25 cm. + Greyish-white, laminated fissured chalk
(After Muckenhausen)

Brown calcareous soils are characteristically formed over Jurassic limestones in Britain, but they are also described from Africa, America, and other areas of the world. These soils develop on limestones with a larger insoluble residue, and therefore they become deeper than the rendzina having a Bw horizon developed between the A horizon with its mull humus and the limestone C horizon. The A horizon is usually dark reddish-brown, crumb structured and moderately rich in organic matter, with a neutral or slightly acid reaction. The Bw horizon is distinguished by a more ochreous coloration caused by stable iron

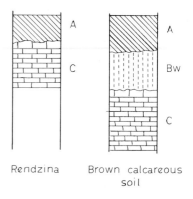

10.1 Diagrammatic profiles of rendzina and brown calcareous soils

compounds. Although these soils are deeper than the rendzinas, they are seldom more than 75 cm. from the surface to the rock beneath. This gives them greater moisture reserves, and they are considered to be good agricultural soils in England.

Profile of a brown calcareous soil (Lithic Eutrochrept; Calcic Cambisol) from Nottinghamshire, England
(Parent material – Permian limestone)

Ap 0–23 cm. Dark reddish-brown (5YR3/2) sandy loam with occasional angular fragments of limestone and rounded quartzite stones; fine to medium sub-angular blocky structure; friable; moderate amount intimate organic matter; abundant fibrous roots; sharp boundary

Bw 23–35 cm. Reddish-brown (5YR4/2) sandy clay loam with occasional fragments of limestone and rounded quartzite stones; weak medium sub-angular blocky structure; friable; organic matter confined to earthworm channels; calcareous; sharp boundary

C 35 cm. + Weathering limestone
(After Bridges)

Because of their shallowness, both rendzinas and brown calcareous soils may not have supported dense vegetation in the past. In Britain, the rendzina is typical of the downland of south-east England, but examples can be seen also where erosion has reduced the depth of soils on other limestones. Areas of brown calcareous soils in Britain were probably scrub woodland until relatively recent times, and many limestone districts still bear the name 'heath' as in the county of Lincolnshire. It is only in relatively recent times that these soils have proved to be excellent arable soils.

Many, but not all, soils of desert areas are calcareous as leaching is insufficient to remove completely all calcium carbonate. Calcic horizons have developed where soft forms of carbonate accumulate; hard forms of petrocalcic horizons do not correlate with present rainfall amounts and are considered to be relic features. Most pedologists symbolise the calcareous nature of certain horizons by the subscript ca (Bca or Cca) but some American authors have suggested a K horizon where carbonate material is in excess of 50 per cent. Where erosion reveals the petrocalcic horizon at the surface it has been called calcrete or *croûte calcaire*.

In humid tropical conditions, calcium carbonate becomes depleted rapidly from parent materials and rocks. Tower karst and pinnacles of limestone are common geomorphological phenomena where a soil cover is completely lacking. On limestone crests in Malaysia shallow, acid, highly humose soils have been noted. On gentler slopes between limestone outcrops clay-rich soils (Ustalfs; Acrisols, Nitosols) are developed. Other base-rich parent materials and rocks in humid tropical climates have been observed strongly to influence the soils and forests growing upon them. Studies in the Solomon Islands and in New Caledonia have revealed toxic levels of heavy metals and high levels of magnesium which interfere with normal growth. In all cases there are low amounts of nitrogen and phosphorus which limit growth.

Hydromorphic soils

Poor drainage can be observed in the soils of most regions of the world and as such represents the most widely spread of the processes of soil formation, leading to the formation of *gley* or *hydromorphic soils*. Often these soils are analogous with soils of similar parent material on freely drained positions of the landscape, and a complete range from freely drained to poorly drained soils can be seen (Fig. 11.3). Hydromorphic soils can be found in association with all zonal soils, anywhere in fact where water can gather together in sufficient volume and for sufficient time to produce the effects of gleying.

Gleying occurs when water saturates a soil, filling all the pore spaces and driving out the air. Any remaining oxygen is soon used by the micro-biological population, and anaerobic conditions are established. At the same time, the soil water contains the decomposition products of organic matter. In the reducing conditions brought about by the absence of oxygen and in the presence of organic matter, iron compounds are chemically reduced from the ferric to the ferrous state. In the ferrous form iron is very much more soluble, and is removed from the soil leaving behind the colourless minerals. This gives gley soils their characteristic grey coloration.

Hydromorphic soils can be sub-divided into those which have continuously saturated conditions, and those which have only a temporary period of saturation. Generally, this division distinguishes those soils with a permanent water-table within the soil from those that are slowly permeable. European pedologists have referred to the former as *gley soils*, and the latter as *pseudo-gley soils*. In Britain these have been called *ground-water gley* and *surface water gley* soils.

There are differences of opinion regarding the classification of poorly drained soils. In the U.S. Soil Taxonomy they become widely dispersed throughout the suborders as Aquents, Aqualfs, Aquox, etc. In the World Soil Map Legend hydromorphic soils occur as Gleysols formed in unconsolidated materials, or as gleyic soils of other map units. Definition of individual classification units is complex and for full details the appropriate sources must be consulted. Although individual criteria may vary, the basic features of hydromorphism include saturation by groundwater so the capilliary fringe reaches the soil surface, dominant grey colours, evidence of the reduction and segregation of iron and the presence of a peaty surface horizon.

Surface-water gley soils are those in which the drainage is impeded above an impervious or very slowly permeable sub-soil horizon (Fig. 10.2 and Plate 29). This leads to the development of grey colours along the fissures and pores of the soil, particularly in the B horizon and the lower parts of the E horizon. Usually these soils are deve-

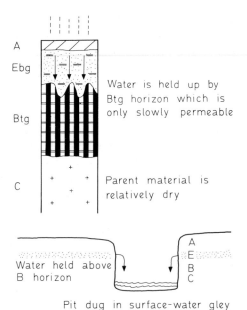

Water is held up by Btg horizon which is only slowly permeable

Parent material is relatively dry

Water held above B horizon

Pit dug in surface-water gley fills with water by seepage down pit sides

10.2 Diagrammatic profile of a surface-water gley soil

10.3 Diagrammatic profile of a ground-water gley soil

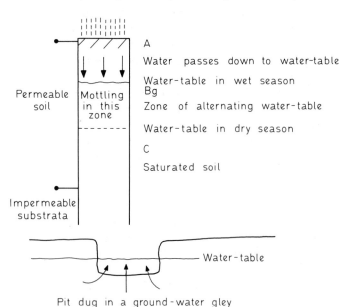

Permeable soil

Mottling in this zone

Impermeable substrata

A
Water passes down to water-table

Water-table in wet season
Bg
Zone of alternating water-table

Water-table in dry season
C
Saturated soil

Water-table

Pit dug in a ground-water gley fills with water by water rising to level of water-table in the soil

loped from fine-grained parent materials in which clay movement has taken place to form a textural B horizon. However, not all surface-water gley soils have clay skins in their B horizons, and the calcareous gley soils in particular differ from them in this way.

Profile of a surface-water gley soil (Haplaquept, Gleyic Cambisol) from Derbyshire, England
(Parent material – glacial drift)

L		Discontinuous litter of beech, sycamore and oak leaves
F	2.5–0.5 cm.	Comminuted leaf fragments, darker and more humified towards the base of the horizon
H	0.5–0.0 cm.	Black amorphous humus
A	0.0–1.5 cm.	Very dark grey (10YR3/1) stoneless sandy loam with bleached sand grains; medium sub-angular blocky structure; friable; high amount organic matter; abundant fibrous roots; narrow irregular boundary
Eb	1.5–23 cm.	Brown (10YR5/3) slightly stony sandy clay loam with medium sub-angular blocky structure; common woody roots; narrow boundary
Ebg	23–35 cm.	Mottled yellowish-brown (10YR5/4) to strong brown (7.5YR5/8), with greyish-brown (10YR5/2) on structure faces; slightly stony sandy clay loam with medium angular blocky structure; firm; low amount organic matter, few roots; earthy iron and manganese concretions; narrow boundary
Bg	35–75 cm.	Dark brown (7.4YR4/4) mottled to pale olive (5YR6/3) on structure faces; slightly stony clay with coarse prismatic structure; firm, plastic when wet; low amount organic matter, few roots; black manganiferous patterning; merging boundary
Cg	75 cm. +	Dark brown (7.5YR4/4) mottled to pale olive (5YR6/3) stony firm clay with structure no longer obvious; firm, plastic when wet; no visible organic matter, no roots; slightly calcareous

(After Bridges)

Most gley soils may become aerated occasionally in the event of a prolonged drought. As a result they may have the colours of ferric iron compounds present as a mottling in the Bg horizons. Gleying can best be seen along the fissures and pores where the effects are most concentrated; the internal parts of the peds often remain aerated and in the ferric state. In the A horizon of most gley soils, grass roots frequently become coated with iron in the form of rusty sheaths.

Ground-water gley soils include those in which there is a water-table which rises to within 60 cm. of the soil surface (Fig. 10.3). Usually these soils are formed from rather permeable parent materials such as alluvial sands and gravels which overlie an impervious sub-stratum upon which water accumulates. Therefore, these soils occur in the lower parts of the landscape and are often transitional to organic soils. In the natural state these soils have well-developed grey colours brought about by the continual anaerobic conditions, but as many of these have been artificially drained mottling can frequently be seen.

Halomorphic soils

In semi-arid and arid parts of the world soils are developed under the influence of soluble salts or with sodium as the dominant exchangeable cation. These are classified as halomorphic soils. The presence of soluble salts or exchangeable sodium exerts an adverse effect upon the growth of most crops producing specific physical features in the soils. As salty soils usually occur in lowland alluvial sites, they coincide with potentially fertile and adequately watered areas.

In common with other soils, classification of halomorphic soils in the U.S. Soil Taxonomy is completed by reference to a diagnostic horizon. Accumulation of secondary salts, at least 2 per cent and in a horizon 15 cm. thick, constitutes a salic horizon. A gypsic horizon possesses at least 5 per cent more calcium sulphate than the underlying material. Where the exchange capacity is more than 15 per cent saturated with sodium ions and the horizon possesses also the properties of an argillic horizon, it is referred to as a natric horizon. Although these features most commonly appear in great groups of the Aridisols, they can also be found in great groups of the Mollisols and Alfisols.

An alternative method of measuring salt content is through the electrical conductivity of a saturation extract from the soil. In the F.A.O./U.N.E.S.C.O. World Soil Map, solonchaks are those soils with a saturation extract of more than 15 mmhos* per cm. in a horizon within 125 cm. from the surface. Solonchaks with salic horizons and solonetz with natric horizons are separate units, but gypsic Yermosols and Xerosols form the upland or non-hydromorphic forms of halomorphic soils.

Halomorphic soils occur in all continents as discontinuous patches within other major soil groups. As they do not form a zonal type of their own, they are classified with the intrazonal soils (Plate 30). Two conditions are necessary for salt accumulation in soils; firstly, a dry climate in which salts are not leached out and secondly, a parent material or ground-water which contains salt. The salt can be derived from rock salt or from the weathering of sodium silicates. Alternatively, salt can be obtained from salt spray which is driven inland into an arid area and not leached away. Soils can undergo a secondary enrichment of salt by artificially raising the water-table so that water can evaporate from the soil surface, leaving salts behind. Examples of the secondary enrichment of soils have occurred in the Indus Valley, Pakistan and in California, U.S.A. In these and other areas affected by salts, either crops are reduced in yield or the land is eventually abandoned as being useless. Remedial action is often practicable, but in many cases is not financially possible.

The salts which affect soils are chiefly the sulphates, chlorides and carbonates of sodium and magnesium. Salts can be present either as an electrolyte in the soil solution or as cations which occupy exchange positions on the clay-humus complex. Soils in which there are concentrations of neutral salts, such as sodium sulphate or sodium chloride, have a lower pH value, generally less than pH 8. Although sodium is present, dispersion does not take place. The soils are reasonably well structured. They may have an efflorescence of salt on the surface during the dry season, a feature which gave them their previous

*The unit of measurement for conductivity is the mho, the reciprocal of the ohm used to measure electrical resistance.

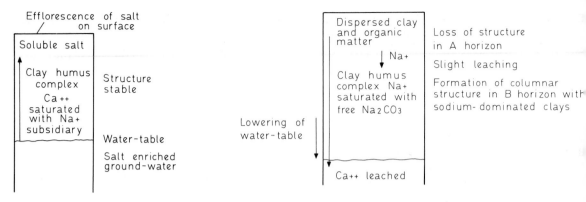

10.4 Solonchak soils. Salts are carried into the soil by salt enriched ground-water. The water evaporates from the surface leaving a salt crust

10.5 Solonetz soils. Lowering of the ground-water enables loss of calcium, this results in saturation by sodium alone and instability of structure

American name – *white alkali soils*. This type of soil is equally well known as solonchak, the Russian name for these soils (Fig. 10.4).

Profile of a solonchak soil (Calciorthid; Orthic Solonchak) from Kayseri, Turkey
(Parent material – lacustrine alluvium)

0.5– 0.0 cm.	White (10YR8/2), dry salt crust
0.0– 20 cm.	Pale brown (8YR6/3) very weak granular or structureless silty clay; friable; hard when dry; strongly calcareous; gradual boundary
22– 55 cm.	Same colour and texture; firm, hard, rounded vesicular aggregates about 1.5 cm. diameter; strongly calcareous with numerous salt crystals and eyes or spots of salts
55–105 cm.	White (5Y8/2) silty clay; saturated below 80 cm. – apparently level of water-table at time of sampling

(After Oakes)

Alkaline soils may be formed from solonchak by leaching initiated by a fall in the water-table, increased rainfall or irrigation. As the leaching of sodium ions from the soil includes some special reactions, the process has been given the name of *solodization*. The soluble salts are easily washed out, and if the soil is dominated by calcium ions, it reverts to the soil appropriate to its region – a chernozem or chestnut soil. If the soil is dominated by sodium ions, there is a loss of stability so that the surface horizons become structureless with dispersed humus and clay. This gives these

soils a dark-coloured appearance which caused them to be called *black alkali soils* (Fig. 10.5). Alternatively known by their Russian name of *solonetz*, these soils have a high pH value brought about by the presence of sodium carbonate in the soil according to the following reaction:

$$Na\ clay + H_2O \rightarrow H\ clay + NaOH$$
$$2NaOH + CO_2 \rightarrow Na_2CO_3 + H_2O$$

Hydrogen ions from rainwater displace sodium ions from the exchange positions forming acid clays, and sodium hydroxide appears in the soil solution. Carbon dioxide is present in the soil, released from plant roots and bacteria; it combines with the sodium hydroxide to form sodium carbonate which raises the pH value to pH 9 or greater. The dispersed clay and humus move down the profile which leads to the development of a surface horizon which is dark grey. Below this is a light grey platy or structureless eluvial horizon which overlies an extremely intractable clay B horizon arranged in the columnar structures so typical of these soils (Plate 31).

Profile of a solonetz soil (Natrargid; Solonetz) from the Hunter Valley, N.S.W. Australia
(Parent material – river terrace deposits)

A	0– 8 cm.	Dark to very dark greyish-brown (10YR4/2) friable silt loam with thin platy structure
A$_2$	8–15 cm.	Pinkish-grey (7.5YR7/3) friable silt loam with thin platy structure

B₁	15–28 cm.	Dark brown (7.5YR3/2) columnar clay with columns weakly rounded at the top and slightly degraded. Columns are 6 to 10 cm. in diameter
B₂	28–75 cm.	Very dark brown (10YR2/2) heavy hard clay with very coarsely irregular blocky structure, very plastic and sticky when wet
B₃	75 cm. +	Very dark greyish-brown (10YR3/2) crumbly clay which is plastic and sticky when wet and contains hard calcium carbonate concretions 0.5 cm. in diameter

(After Thorp)

There is a complete range of soils from the solonetz to a soil which is completely free of sodium ions. The intermediate soils are known as *solodized solonetz* and the completely leached soil is known as a *solod*. The A horizons of the solodized solonetz are deeper and they possess caps of amorphous silica on top of the columnar structures of the B horizon. This solodization process is evident from the description of the solonetz soil given above when the columns are described as being slightly degraded. When the complete removal of sodium ions is achieved, the soil becomes acid, the structure stabilises, and cultivation is again possible (Fig. 10.6). Unfortunately the amelioration of these soils is patchy in occurrence and a uniform reclamation is difficult to obtain as halomorphic features persist in the lower-lying parts of the landscape.

10.6 Solod soil. Complete leaching results in a solod soil which is acid and moderately well structured.
1. Leaching of organic matter.
2. Leaching of calcium ions.
3. Leaching of soluble salts

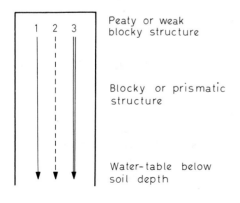

Profile of a solod soil (Aqualf; Gleyic Cambisol) from Askania Nova, Ukraine
(Parent material – redistributed loess-like loams)

A₁	0– 10 cm.	Grey, just moist medium loam with platy structure; friable and non-calcareous; gradual boundary
A₂	10– 30 cm.	Pallid grey medium loam with platy structure; friable and non-calcareous; sharp boundary
A₂Bg	30– 40 cm.	Greyish-olive-green medium loam with nutty-prismatic structure compact and non-calcareous; iron-manganese concretions; gradual boundary
Cg	100–230 cm.	Olive-green clay; very compact and plastic; abundant iron-manganese concretions. From 130 cm. compact calcareous concretions

(After Grin and Kissel)

In several parts of semi-arid Australia salting has occurred on the lower slopes and valley bottoms as the result of the interference in the landscape by man. Removal of the original forest resulted in an increased rate of removal of salts from the soils of the interfluve areas, but the rainfall is not sufficient to flush the salt right away. Consequently, it accumulates in the valley bottom lands rendering them unsuitable for most plants.

Knowledge of halomorphic soils has been of use in areas outside the desert and semi-desert regions of the world. Reclamation of the soils of the polders of Holland has necessitated treatment for the effects of salts.

Andosols

Other soils which are worthy of mention include the *Andosols*, which are named from soils developed on recent base-rich volcanic deposits in Japan. These soils are also intrazonal in that they occur in many different zones from Alaska in the tundra to tropical Africa and Indonesia. Their colour is dark brown and they have a thick friable, organic-rich A horizon overlying a Bw horizon which shows little development of clay movement. The Andosols have a low bulk density and they are not sticky. Classification of these soils according to the U.S. Soil Taxonomy results in them being placed in the Inceptisols as Andepts.

The World Soil Map Legend retains the name Andosols. *Brown soils* are also described from Africa where they occur on recent volcanic ash, basic rocks or alluvial deposits. As these are relatively young soils, they contain a reserve of weatherable minerals, and their clays are montmorillonitic. Although not extensive in area, these are fertile soils used for crops of bananas, cocoa and coffee, though their position on steep slopes often limits their usefulness.

Azonal soils

Azonal soils may be found within any of the zonal soil distributions and can be distinguished from them and from the intrazonal soils in that they lack well-developed soil characteristics. Some factor such as youthfulness, the parent material

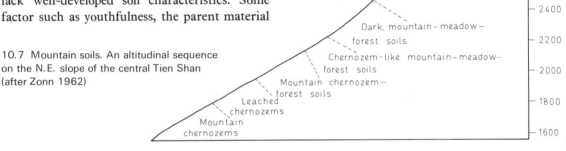

10.7 Mountain soils. An altitudinal sequence on the N.E. slope of the central Tien Shan (after Zonn 1962)

or relief has prevented the development of well-defined pedological features. In all cases these soils lack a B horizon, and the thin rudimentary A horizon is only distinguished from the C horizon by the presence of organic matter. Immature soils have caused problems in previous soil classifications which dealt with mature soils only. However, recent attempts have established positions for azonal soils in a world classification. In the U.S. Soil Taxonomy these soils are included in the order Entisols, but their definition includes lithosols, regosols, alluvial soils as well as thin rankers.

Lithosols develop at high altitudes where resistant parent materials withstand the disruptive forces of weathering. Soil information is slight, resulting in a humus-enriched shallow soil which is stony with very little fine earth. The lithosols are found in exposed sites where natural erosion is active, such as in mountain areas. All early stages of soil formation leading to *rendzinas* on calcareous parent materials and to *rankers* on non-calcareous parent materials can be considered as lithosols.

Regosols are developed upon deeper, uncon-solidated parent materials such as dune sands or volcanic ash. Elementary profile development takes place rapidly through the highly permeable sand, and although superficial organic horizons may form as well as an A horizon, these soils lack any illuvial horizons. Because of the mobility of the parent material, multiple profiles may be seen where fresh material has accumulated over an already existing regosol profile. Deeper coarse-textured soils in humid tropical regions with insufficient development of horizon characteristics for Ferralsols (Oxisols) are referred to as Arenosols in the World Soil Map Legend or Quartzipsamments in Soil Taxonomy (see p. 86).

Alluvial soils (Fluvaquents; Fluvisols) are variable in texture, drainage and state of maturity. They are liable to flooding and the surface receives fresh additions of material which are laid down in successive layers, often of different grain sizes. Some alluvial soils are poorly drained, even peaty, but others on levees and terraces are imperfectly or freely drained. As they are water-deposited, many alluvial soils retain their layered nature, but older terrace soils gradually achieve maturity and come to resemble adjacent upland soils.

Alluvial soils in many parts of the world have been altered and cultivated by man from very early times. In tropical regions, paddy fields have been constructed from river alluvia, in desert regions irrigation has been practised, and in temperate regions the level of alluvial land has been raised by encouraging artificial sedimentation, a process known as *warping*. Marine alluvia can be reclaimed from the sea, but with these there is the added problem of leaching out the salt from the newly embanked sea-marsh. It has been found necessary to mix different layers of sediment to form a reasonable soil texture in some of the Dutch polders.

Mountain soils

The soils of mountainous regions are frequently shallow and subject to erosion on steep slopes. Different aspects can have a considerable influence upon the soil profile developed on either side of a valley. The increased altitude brings different climate and vegetation formations, so it can be expected that soils will also occur in altitudinal zones in mountainous areas. Several writers have described sequences from different parts of the world including the Big Horn Mountains of America which have a sequence of grey desert soils, brown desert soils, chestnut soils, chernozems, prairie soils and podzolic soils. A similar sequence is given for the Tien Shan Mountains, which passes from the chernozems to the snow-line (Fig. 10.7). In the tropics, a sequence from ferrallitic soils (Oxisols; Ferralsols) on the shore of Lake Tanganyika to the snow-line is given in Fig. 10.8.

An altitudinal sequence of soils up to 1770 m. has been described from Central Malaya which is paralleled by similar sequences in Sabah and New Guinea. On the lowlands beneath tropical rainforest yellow latosols (Orthox; Xanthic Ferralsols) are developed. Above 750 m. a lower montane rainforest becomes dominant with humic latosols (Humox; Orthic and Humic Ferralsols) which become increasingly peaty with elevation. Above 1500 m. peaty gley podzols (Placaquods; Placic Podzols) and peat develop where extensive cloud and continual moist conditions occur associated with upper montane rainforest.

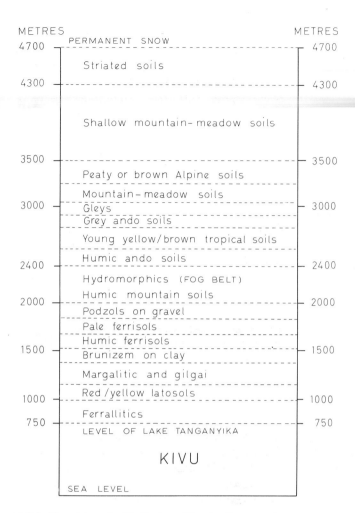

10.8 Mountain soils. Vertical zonality of soils on Kivu, East Africa

Organic soils

Hydromorphic and halomorphic soils are both developed on poorly drained sites, often in association with organic soils (Histosols) on very poorly drained sites. An arbitrary boundary between true peats and the peaty mineral soils is usually drawn where the peat depth exceeds 38 cm. in Britain, but elsewhere other depths are used. Knowledge about organic soils is not plentiful, but the evidence available suggests the division into acid and alkaline or neutral peats. Peats can also be classified according to the site in which they are developed.

Accumulation of organic matter is encouraged by wet conditions; these result from heavy rainfall, seepage or flooding, and high levels of

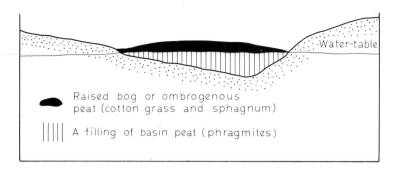

Raised bog or ombrogenous
peat (cotton grass and sphagnum)

A filling of basin peat (phragmites)

10.9 Basin and raised peat formation

ground-water. Where rainfall is generally in excess of 1500 mm. per annum in the uplands of Britain, *blanket bog* peats are favoured, while *raised bog* occurs in wet sites on the lowlands. As both of these forms are above the water-level, they rely entirely upon rainwater for their supply of moisture. Seepage waters and high ground-waters are responsible for the accumulation of lowland peat forms. Different water-levels in the past have resulted in different types of peat developing in any specific area. These may be peats formed from a reed-swamp community of *Phragmites*, or carr peat which has included within it woody fragments of birch, alder and willow which were able to grow in slightly drier conditions. Raised bog and blanket bog peats frequently have formed from a *Sphagnum-Eriophorum* community of plants (Fig. 10.9).

The most important form of lowland peat is *fen peat* which is developed where base-rich waters are associated with an accumulation of organic matter. Peat with a neutral or slightly acid reaction gradually develops as in the fens of England. Fen peat is characteristically black or very dark brown and there are few recognisable plant remains preserved in it.

Acid lowland peats can be formed in places with drainage from non-calcareous rocks; in Britain examples can be found in Lancashire and Somerset. Where rainfall is sufficient raised bog can develop overlying both fen and acid lowland peats. Raised bog peat is formed of brown peat with little mineral matter, and a high proportion of recognisable plant remains. It is built up in the form of a low dome and is usually strongly acid in reaction.

On the uplands of western Europe, particularly western France and Britain, blanket bog covers large areas over 300 m. above sea level. Blanket bog often attains a depth of about 150 cm., although deeper accumulations can be found in declivities. It is black, strongly acid and consists of few identifiable plant remains with very little mineral matter included (Plate 32). It supports a growth of cotton grass and sphagnum moss, but with drainage ditches heather may become dominant and the area can then be grazed.

While the upland peat moors are of little agricultural value because of their extreme wetness and acidity, lowland peat areas are valuable and versatile agricultural and horticultural land. Liming can cure the acidity but this may bring trace element deficiencies into evidence.

11   SOIL MAPPING

As a natural resource, soil and its distribution is of national interest. The more that is known about its distribution and formation, the more it will be used profitably for the individual and the community. Many countries of the world, including Britain, now possess a soil survey organisation which is charged with finding out the distribution, genesis and properties of soils. From this basic work stems a range of applied uses for pedological knowledge (Chapter 12). Agriculture is the most obvious in that a greater knowledge of the soil will help with decisions about crops, cultivations and fertiliser treatments. Where soils have been maltreated the most effective methods of restoration can be explored and used, as has been the case in the opencast workings for coal and iron in many countries. Natural disasters such as the flooding of arable land by salt water which occurred on the east coast of Britain in 1953, can be combated more effectively if something is known about the nature and distribution of the soils affected. Engineering scientists are interested in the physical properties of the soil for construction of roads, buildings and embankments. In the developing countries change from an agricultural system of low productivity to a more advanced form necessitates advance knowledge of the soils, particularly where the installation of expensive irrigation projects is being considered.

Until the production of the F.A.O./ U.N.E.S.C.O. World Soil Map, world soil maps were based essentially on the prevailing environmental conditions, therefore they strongly reflected the patterns seen in the climate and vegetation maps. If the general conditions of soil formation are similar in two given areas, then a specific soil will be produced in both areas. Thus these maps do not always show the actual soils, but only the most probable zonal soil which might occur. These maps show tundra soils, podzols, chernozems, desert soils, etc. (Fig. 11.1). For example, most world soil maps generalise the British Isles into a northwest zone of podzols, and a southeast zone of brown earths. This gross over-simplification emerges when it is realised that some of the best developed podzols actually occur in the south and east of England. In producing a world soil map, the process of mapping is carried out at an empirical level, using the climate. Of necessity the scale of such maps prohibits the inclusion of local detail. World maps convenient for reproduction in atlases are usually at scales of about 1 : 80,000,000 at which only the broadest generalisations can be shown. For general purposes of geographical interpretation it is desirable to have maps of a country or region which show a moderate amount of detail. This becomes possible at scales of 1 : 5,000,000 and larger. A successful soil map of Africa was published in 1964 and at the time of writing several sheets of the F.A.O./U.N.E.S.C.O. Soil Map of the World have been published at a scale of 1 : 5,000,000. The nomenclature and legend for this map is referred to constantly throughout this book as the F.A.O./U.N.E.S.C.O. World Soil Map represents the most authoritative available compilation of world soil distribution. The authors of the Soil Map of the World state that their soil units are generally comparable to the 'great group' level in the U.S. Soil Taxonomy.

In the past, two groupings of soils have been used on maps of medium scale, the *catena* and the *soil association*. The catena was used by Milne for mapping soils in East Africa, where he found a regularly occurring relationship of the soils with topographic features. The type of relationship can be seen from Fig. 11.2. It has been found to be most useful in mapping large areas of similar parent material within a uniform climatic regime.

In a similar manner, the Scottish soil scientists have grouped topographically related soils deve-

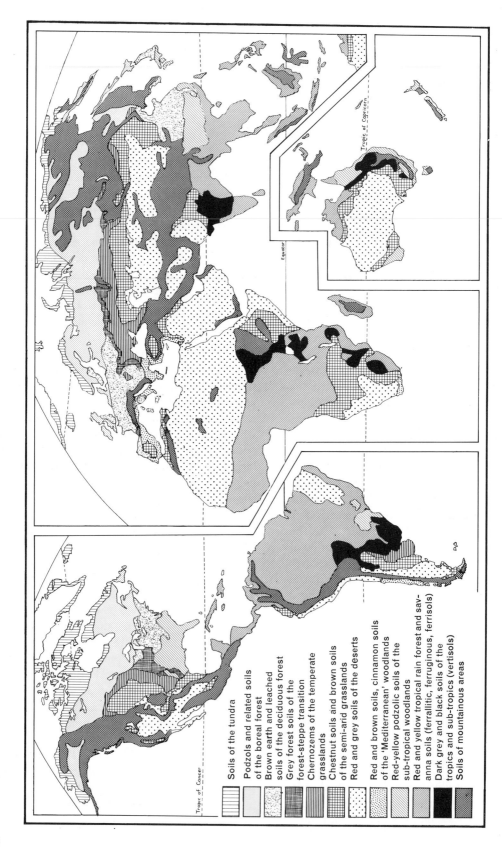

Soils of the tundra

Podzols and related soils
of the boreal forest

Brown earth and leached
soils of the deciduous forest

Grey forest soils of the
forest-steppe transition

Chernozems of the temperate
grasslands

Chestnut soils and brown soils
of the semi-arid grasslands

Red and grey soils of the deserts

Red and brown soils, cinnamon soils
of the 'Mediterranean' woodlands

Red-yellow podzolic soils of the
sub-tropical woodlands

Red and yellow tropical rain forest and savanna soils (ferrallitic, ferruginous, ferrisols)

Dark grey and black soils of the
tropics and sub-tropics (vertisols)

Soils of mountainous areas

11.1 Simplified world soil map

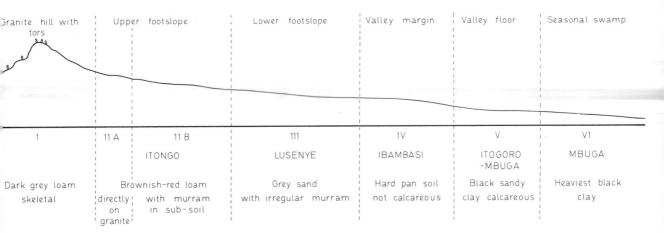

Granite hill with tors	Upper footslope		Lower footslope	Valley margin	Valley floor	Seasonal swamp
1	11 A	11 B	111	1V	V	V1
	ITONGO		LUSENYE	IBAMBASI	ITOGORO -MBUGA	MBUGA
Dark grey loam skeletal	directly on granite	Brownish-red loam with murram in sub-soil	Grey sand with irregular murram	Hard pan soil not calcareous	Black sandy clay calcareous	Heaviest black clay

11.2 In a soil catena a number of different soils are linked together by their relationship to each other on the landscape (murram is lateritic gravel)

loped on one geological parent material into a *soil association* (Fig. 11.3). In this case, a catena of soils, based on their inherent drainage properties is made up of a number of soil series. Hence the Ettrick Association derived from Silurian greywackes and shales has six component series in the Jedburgh and Morebattle district:

Freely drained	Linhope series	brown earth
	Dod series	peaty podzol
Poorly drained	Ettrick series	non-calcareous gley
	Alemoor series	peaty gley
Very poorly drained	Peden series	non-calcareous gley
	Hardlee series	peaty gley

For reconnaissance work it is convenient to describe the soils of an area collectively, so a slightly different interpretation of the term association is used. In describing the soils which occur on a geographical tract a number of different soils are *associated* in a landscape, even though they may have completely different processes operating in their formation. In the case of the Carboniferous Limestone of central

11.3 A drainage association on a permeable parent material

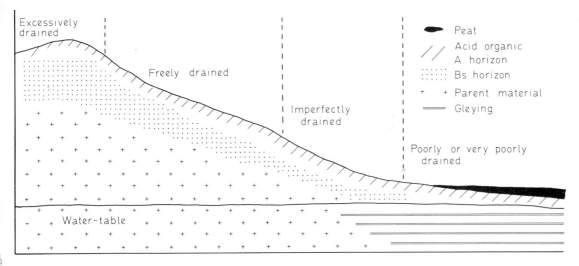

Peat

Acid organic A horizon

Bs horizon

+ + Parent material

Gleying

Excessively drained

Freely drained

Imperfectly drained

Poorly or very poorly drained

Water-table

(3) Napperby Land System (1000 sq. miles)

Granite hills and plains with lower rugged country in a strip from Aileron to west of Mt. Doreen homestead.

Geology.—Massive granite and gneiss, some schist. Pre-Cambrian age, Arunta block, Mt. Doreen–Reynolds Range; Lower Proterozoic, Warramunga geosyncline.

Geomorphology.—Erosional weathered land surface: hills up to 500 ft high and plains with branching shallow valleys; less extensive rugged ridges with relief up to 50 ft, and a dense rectangular pattern of narrow steep-sided valleys.

Water Resources.—Isolated alluvial or fracture aquifers may yield supplies of ground water. There are areas suitable for surface catchments.

Climate.—Nearest comparable climatic station is Tea Tree Well.

Unit	Area	Land Form	Soil*	Plant Community
1	Large	Granite hills: tors and domes up to 500 ft high; bare rock summits, and rectilinear boulder-covered hill slopes, 40–60%, with minor gullies; short colluvial aprons, 5–10%	Outcrop with pockets of shallow, gritty or stony soils	Sparse shrubs and low trees over sparse forbs and grasses, *Triodia spicata*, or *Plectrachne pungens* (spinifex)
2	Medium	Closely-set gneiss ridges and quartz reefs: up to 50 ft high; short rocky slopes, 10–35%; narrow intervening valleys		
3	Medium	Interfluves: up to 20 ft high and ½ mile wide; flattish or convex crests, and concave marginal slopes attaining 2%	Mainly red earths (4*a*), locally red clayey sands (3*a*), and texture-contrast soils (7*a*), stony soils near hills	Sparse low trees over short grasses and forbs or *Eragrostis eriopoda* (woollybutt)
4	Medium	Erosional plains: up to 1 mile in extent, slopes generally less than 1%		
5	Small	Drainage floors: 200–400 yd wide, longitudinal gradients about 1 in 200	Mainly texture-contrast soils (7*e*), locally alluvial soils (1*a*) and red earths	*Eremophila* spp.—*Hakea leucoptera* over short grasses and forbs; minor *Kochia aphylla* (cotton-bush)
6	Small	Alluvial fans: ill-defined distributary drainage; gradients above 1 in 200	Alluvial brown sands (1*a*) and red clayey sands (3*d*)	Sparse low trees over short grasses and forbs or *Aristida browniana* (kerosene grass)
7	Small	Rounded drainage heads: up to 200 yd wide and 5 ft deep on the flanks of unit 3	Red earths	Dense *A. aneura* (mulga) over short grasses and forbs
8	Very small	Channels: up to 50 yd wide and 5 ft deep and braiding locally	Bed-loads mainly coarse grit	*E. camaldulensis* (red gum) – *A. estrophiolata* (ironwood) over *Chloris acicularis* (curly windmill grass)

* The numbers in parentheses in this column refer to soil groupings in Part VIII.

11.4 Reconnaissance mapping of soils can be done by the 'Land System' method

Derbyshire, the associated soils are the Nordrach series, a brown earth; Marian series, a rendzina; and the Ivet series, a brown earth with gleying. These groupings of soils are essentially a regional grouping, bounded by geomorphic elements of the landscape. This is the more common use of the term soil association, which is in effect the association of two or more soil series conveniently grouped together to suit the scale of mapping. When landscape units and their total environment, including geology, geomorphology, soils and vegetation, are mapped such a mapping unit is called a *land system* (Fig. 11.4).

Detailed surveys published at scales of 1:50,000 and larger necessitate the examination of the soil at frequent intervals over the landscape so that the profile characteristics are known and the boundaries between them drawn. The normal procedure is first to make a reconnaisance of the area to find the range of soils present. Once the framework is established, it is possible to begin mapping individual soils as mapping units. These mapping units can then be classified into the named soils series or soil complexes which occur in the area being mapped. In Britain, the *soil series* was defined by G. W. Robinson as follows: 'soils with similar profiles derived from similar material under similar conditions of development are conveniently grouped together as a series'.

Where the pattern of different soil series becomes too complicated and it is deemed uneconomic to map out tiny individual areas of each soil the whole area can be mapped as a *soil complex*. For example, on steep slopes, the variability of parent material and drainage can be considerable, causing a most complicated soil pattern.

Several approaches to detailed mapping are possible, the first method is to observe the soil at fixed points by a grid pattern surveyed over the landscape. This is a method that can be used at a very detailed scale, for example when a field is being surveyed before an agricultural experiment is laid down. In this case the soil would be examined at a close interval of 25 or 50 m., the observations made and the boundaries drawn by interpolation. A similar method of survey is adopted in the case of well-wooded country when it is impossible to locate accurately the position of observations by other means. In West Africa, survey lines are followed and the soil described and sampled at intervals of 200 m. along survey lines 800 m. apart. Supplementary information is obtained from lines at 100 m. interval. This method has been used in the production of soil maps at 1:250,000 in West Africa and the information gained was used to lay out plantations. The production of semi-detailed maps such as these often entails a certain amount of basic survey, as well as observations on the hydrology, vegetation and present land use.

The second method, 'free survey', is a more interpretative approach in which the morphology of the landscape is used to elucidate the soil pattern. Depending upon the 'lie of the land' the soil is inspected with spade or screw auger and the resulting information marked upon a field map. The 1:10,000 maps of the Ordnance Survey are

11.5 Example of detailed soil mapping

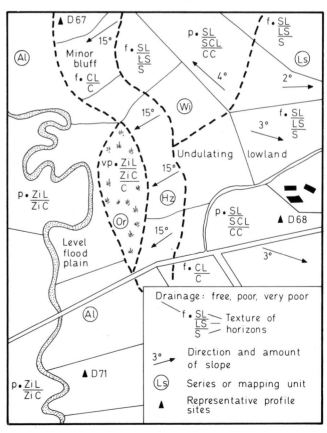

the most convenient for routine mapping at a detailed scale in Britain; where detailed maps are unavailable, air photographs can be used as base maps instead. The soil colour, texture, drainage characteristics and any other notable features are recorded (Fig. 11.5). The boundary between different soil-mapping units is frequently found to follow pronounced morphological breaks of slope in the landscape which aids their location on the map. As the geomorphology often gives a clue to the origin of the parent material upon which the soil is developed, so the particular soil associated with the deposit of geological nature has a boundary which coincides with its areal distribution.

A third method is to follow a boundary, crossing and recrossing it until its position is accurately known. This is a time-consuming activity and the results are not materially better than those achieved by interpretative methods of mapping. It is a method which has to be adopted when other features such as vegetation and morphology of the land cannot be interpreted. Fortunately, there are very few areas of the world which are featureless, so the surveyor usually has some other data to guide him in his map compilation.

A fourth method, also interpretative, uses the information contained upon monochrome air photographs. Without going into the details of air-photo interpretation, an appreciation of relief can be obtained from stereoscopic examination. The tone of the print together with its texture, gives a good impression of the variation of the colour of the soil or of the vegetation growing upon it. Consequently, a skilled interpreter can see the distribution of both vegetation and soil and mark the boundaries on the photograph. This is made possible by the reaction of plants to different soil conditions. It is then an essential second stage of the survey to go out into the field and to examine the soil within the areas determined from the air photograph to see if they are truly representative of the vegetation patterns which they support. Recent developments in air photography have used colour and other sensory methods to map soil distributions.

A skilled soil surveyor uses all the information which is available. This includes not only the soil itself, but the breaks and changes in the slope of the land, the geology of the parent material, the vegetation which grows naturally, including hedgerows in arable areas, as well as the present land use. However, in the latter case utilization can be dictated by purely economic considerations which are not always in the best interests of soil conservation and good farming.

Once the different soil-mapping units have been mapped it is usual for the surveyor to dig a hole, make a description and sample the horizons of the proposed profile at selected sites. These bulk samples are placed in waxed paper or polythene bags, labelled and brought back to the laboratory, where analyses can be made of the samples to support the decisions about classifications made in the field. Undisturbed samples can be taken in 'Kubiena Boxes' for micromorphological study, or a monolith of the whole soil profile collected in a galvanised iron trough made specifically for that purpose.

Normally the profile description is entered on a field description sheet where observations about site and soil are recorded. Soil descriptions also may be written out in full in a notebook, recorded on a portable tape recorder or coded in a format suitable for handling by computer on standard soil description cards. Observations are conveniently listed under the headings: general information, site description and profile description.

A General information:
   Profile number
   Grid reference
   Described by
   Date
   Weather
   Locality
B Site description:
   Elevation
   Relief
   Soil erosion and deposition
   Flooding
   Rock outcrops
   Land use and vegetation
   Soil surface

The features listed above are clearly designed to give information about the area in which the soil profile is situated, and the different sections should be answered as fully as possible by the surveyor at the time of description.

Profile description:
Recognition of horizons
Depth of horizons and thickness
Colour
Texture
Stoniness
Structure
Consistence
Soil-water state
Organic matter status
Roots and other soil flora
Fauna
Carbonates
Features of pedogenetic origin
Boundary to next horizon
pH

The above details are given for each of the soil horizons found to occur within the soil profile. The full range of terminology is given, in the case of England and Wales, by the field handbook of the Soil Survey of England and Wales. The terminology used by other countries is similar, but care must be exercised to check the exact use of the terms employed. Measurement in centimetres for the depth of soil horizons is now commonplace and the use of the Munsell colour charts is widely accepted for the description of soil colours. An international range of textures has been agreed upon, and is incorporated into most soil survey systems, but some other measurements for particle size are also used (p. 17).

Once the various horizons of a profile have been described and identified, they are referred to by a system of nomenclature using capital letters with subscripts. This system was originated by Dokuchaiev who simply labelled his soil horizons A, B, C, but eventually these symbols came to have genetic significance as can be seen from the explanation of the symbols in Chapter 1 and the discussion of the processes in Chapter 4.

The tools used by soil surveyors are mostly fairly straightforward and can be supplied by most competent tool shops, or laboratory suppliers (Fig. 11.6). For rapid inspection of the

11.6 Tools of the soil surveyor. Illustrated are two types of auger, spade, trowel and pick-axe for obtaining samples and digging soil-pits. Tape-measures are used for location and for measurement of horizon depths. A mapcase, notebook and soil description card (used in conjunction with the Soil Survey Field Handbook by experienced soil surveyors), Munsell Colour Charts and pH kit are items normally used in the field. Plastic bags and labels are for soil samples to be used in laboratory analysis.

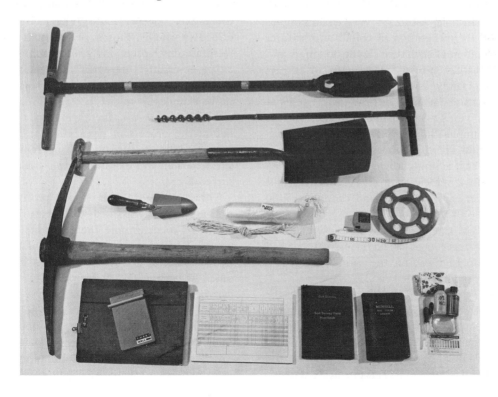

11.7 Landrover with power auger

soil, a screw auger is probably the best tool in that it can be used to remove successive samples from a small hole. Although these small samples are useful for recognition of colour and texture, no appreciation of structure can be obtained, and in dry weather it can be difficult to extract samples of sandy soils from the hole. Similar comments can be made about the Jarrett auger, a larger tool with a 10 cm. diameter bucket. It gives a bigger sample than the screw auger but structure is again difficult to assess as the sample is disrupted as it is brought up. A power-auger can be fitted to a vehicle such as a Landrover, but power-augers are expensive and cannot be used successfully in very stony soils (Fig. 11.7). The larger size of the cylindrical cores removed by the power-auger enables an assessment of soil structure to be made on the sample when it is split down the middle.

Normally, digging a profile pit necessitates the use of a strong spade, and in some cases a pick-axe is essential. A pit should be large enough to obtain the necessary information, and yet not so large that effort is wasted in the removal of a great weight of soil. Most soil pits are 1 m. wide

and 1.5 m. long at the surface, with steps down to successively deeper levels. The face to be described is usually chosen so that it is well lit to facilitate description and photography. A trowel either an ordinary gardener's trowel, or a special sampling trowel, is useful for removing representative samples from the face of a profile pit. The trowel is useful, too, for 'facing-up' the pit side before the process of description and sampling begins. This is the process of removing the smeared soil and exposing fresh structures and surfaces.

Other necessary aids to soil profile description are a clearly marked steel measuring tape, a small kit to determine the pH value of the soil at each horizon, and a small bottle of 10 per cent hydrochloric acid with which to test for the presence of carbonates. A form of map case which can be used for writing upon in the field is essential as this can hold maps and field soil description sheets. Many surveyors find a pocket notebook is useful for recording details of sections, vegetation, land use and other relevant information not easily recorded on the field map.

12 SOIL DISTRIBUTION AND APPLICATIONS OF SOIL SCIENCE

In the past, knowledge about soils has been acquired slowly, and only communicated by word of mouth. The best use of the soil has been evolved by trial and error controlled largely by tradition. However, in recent years the necessity for more planning has become paramount. By the end of the twentieth century the maximum use will have to be made of our soil resources, particularly for the production of food. As yet we have only information of reconnaisance standard about the soils of many parts of the world. Although most countries now undertake some research in pedology and have some form of soil survey, the responsible organisations are usually small bodies with much to do. New developments in the use of remote sensory methods of recording, using infra-red photographs of organic content, heat and moisture content, as well as panchromatic and colour photography, offer the possibility of more rapid mapping techniques in the immediate future. In spite of this it may be two or three hundred years before most countries are mapped in detail; a lamentable situation at a time when demands for food are far outstripping the supply.

Soil distribution and utilisation

The different soil groupings are very unevenly distributed on the land masses of the earth. This is seen readily from the World Soil Map (Fig. 11.1) but an approximate distribution in percentage terms of the individual continents is given in Table 12.1.

In Eurasia the most extensive soil groups are those of the mountain, podzolic and desert groups, with dry subtropical and tropical soils and the

Table 12.1 *Percentage distribution of major soil groups*

	Eurasia	N. America	S. America	Africa	Australia	Per cent total land
Tundra soils	3	17	–	–	–	4
Podzols	16	23	–	–	–	9
Grey and brown forest soils	7	6	8	9	7	7
Chernozems and vertisols	6	7	5	7	4	6
Chestnut and red-brown soils	7	7	6	9	10	7
Desert soils	15	7	3	37	44	17
Ferrallitic soils, ferruginous soils and laterite	9	10	59	29	25	19
Alluvial soils	4	1	7	6	–	4
Mountain soils	33	14	12	3	10	16
Snow and Ice	–	8	–	–	–	2

Table 12.2   *Land area, cultivated and potential arable land*

	Total land area (millions of hectares)	Cultivated land	Potential arable land	% of land area cultivated
Africa	3,010	158	734	5.2
Asia	2,740	519	627	18.9
Australasia	820	32	153	3.9
Europe	480	154	174	32.1
North America	2,110	239	465	11.3
South America	1,750	77	681	4.4
U.S.S.R.	2,240	227	356	10.6
Totals	13,150	1,406	3,190	10.6

Adapted from *The World Food Problem*, U.S. Govt. Printing Office, 1967.

more versatile and productive brown earths and chernozems all occupying less than 10 per cent each. Podzols are most extensive in North America but tundra soils and mountain soils together cover approximately one third of the continent. The more productive soils occupy considerably less than 10 per cent in each category. The overwhelming preponderance of tropical soils in South America is very obvious reflecting the large area of the Amazon basin with ferrallitic and ferruginous soils. In Africa the soil distribution reflects the extent of that continent within the inter-tropical and desert zones. In Australasia the desert soils again dominate but tropical soils are extensive in moister areas.

The proportion of the soils of the world at present utilised for cropping (excluding grazing land) is only between 10 and 11 per cent. This figure includes considerable variation amongst the separate continents ranging from less than 5 per cent in South America to over 30 per cent in Europe (Table 12.2). Many soils at present under cultivation are used at levels well below their potential productive capacity as yields are limited by traditional methods of agriculture and lack of capital for machinery and fertilisers. In the context of the different soil groups, those soils most effectively used at the present time would appear to be the brown earths and andosols, and the groups with the greatest areas at present under-used (land potentially available for cultivation) occur within the soils of the humid tropics, the chernozems and desert soils (Table 12.3)

The total area of potentially available arable land not at present under crops is estimated to be 1,784 million hectares. With the techniques of modern agricultural technology it is estimated that approximately 23 to 25 per cent of the earth's land surface could be arable. The grand total of land at present under arable crops plus the potentially arable land amounts to 3190 million hectares.

Table 12.3   *Total area and potential arable land in soil groups*

	Total area (millions of hectares)	Potential arable land (millions of hectares)
Tundra soils	517	0
Desert soils	2,180	430
Chernozems	822	450
Noncalcic brown soils	291	110
Podzols	1,920	300
Red-yellow podzolic soils	388	130
Ferrallitic and Ferruginous soils	2,500	1,050
Vertisols and terra rossas	325	180
Brown forest soils and Rendzinas	101	30
Andosols	24	10
Lithosols	2,722	80
Regosols	763	70
Alluvial soils	595	350
Total	13,150	3,190

Adapted from *The World Food Problem*, U.S. Govt. Printing Office, 1967

Estimates by Dutch soil scientists based upon the F.A.O./U.N.E.S.C.O. World Soil Map and the potential productivity of soils broadly agree with the American studies of 1967 undertaken by the President's Science Advisory Committee that there is approximately one-quarter of the land surface of the world which can be used as arable land. Not all studies have been so optimistic; a report presented to the Club of Rome took a more pessimistic view of the potential productivity of tropical soils and proposed a potential arable land total only two-thirds of the American and Dutch figures. When it is considered that this is by no means all first class arable land where soil fertility and climatic factors are favourable for a high level of agricultural production, it can be seen that there is a finite limit to food production on the earth. Productivity, assessed in terms of grain equivalents, suggests that the absolute maximum productivity of the world is 49,830 million tons. At present the cereal crop production (1970–72) averages 1268 million tons, or one-fortieth of the maximum possible. Thus, there is considerable scope for expanding agricultural productivity but this requires capital investment in equipment, technology, fertiliser, and particularly in means of marketing and distribution. It is fortunate that those lands most capable of increased productivity are in the developing world for the need for increased food production is greatest in those countries, but unfortunately the necessary finance, expertise and marketing infrastructure are not present. Moreover, changes in agricultural practices inevitably bring changes in the social structure which either are resisted or used for devious financial or political ends.

Land use capability classification

Several attempts have been made to classify land and its capability. Although this might seem to be an obvious and straightforward geographical exercise of some practical value, it is fraught with difficulties because of the many different combinations of soil, site and current economic conditions. Although land-use maps have been used in Britain for planning purposes, they are not based upon the fundamental properties of the land. However, if a land classification is based upon the fundamental properties or limitations

Table 12.4 *The U.S.D.A. land-capability classification*

CLASS I
Soils with few limitations that restrict their use

CLASS II
Soils with some limitations that reduce the choice of plants or require moderate conservation practices

CLASS III
Soils with severe limitations that reduce the choice of plants or require special conservation practices or both

CLASS IV
Soils with very severe limitations that restrict the choice of plants, require very careful management, or both

CLASS V
Soils with little or no erosion hazard but with other limitations impracticable to remove that limit their use largely to pasture, range, woodland, or wildlife food and cover. (In practice used mainly for level valley floors that are swampy or subject to frequent flooding.)

CLASS VI
Soils with very severe limitations that make them generally unsuited to cultivation and limit their use largely to pasture or range, woodland, or wildlife

CLASS VII
Soils with very severe limitations that make them unsuited to cultivation and restrict their use largely to grazing, woodland and wildlife

CLASS VIII
Soils and landforms with limitations that preclude their use for commercial plant production and restrict it to recreation, wildlife, water supply or aesthetic purposes

imposed by the environment, which are not so easily changed, the resulting classification can be interpreted in the light of current economic conditions. Limitations included in this type of soil and landscape assessment include: wetness caused by impermeable or slowly permeable soil horizons, high rainfall or flooding, shallowness, stoniness, extremes of texture and structure and inherent low fertility of the soils, gradient of the land and the soil pattern, liability for erosion, climatic limitations induced by increasing altitude above sea-level and increasing rainfall. Consideration of these limiting factors enables land to be classified on a scale of eight classes in

12.1 A landscape with the land use capability classes and subclasses indicated. Well drained shallow chalky loams (2s), wet clay lowlands (3w) and steep slopes (4g) occur related to the pattern of topography and soils

the U.S.A. (Table 12.4), or seven classes in Great Britain (Table 12.5). In both schemes arable land with diminishing versatility comprises classes I to IV (Fig. 12.1). The remaining classes are concerned with land most suited for grassland, forest and non-agricultural natural reserves.

Within each class, subclasses can be identified according to the limiting factor or factors which detract from them and are given an appropriate symbol. In the British system, five are used: wetness (w), soil (s), gradient (g), climate (c), and erosion (e). It is a classification which is primarily for agricultural purposes, and the land capability is assessed from its use under a moderately high level of management. It does not attempt to state the suitability of the soil and land for specific crops, nor is the distance to markets, availability of roads and farm structure taken into account even though these will effect decisions about the land use. Where limitations can be removed at reasonable cost, the land is graded upon the severity of the remaining limitations. Minor improvement schemes liable to deteriorate with time

Table 12.5 *The land-use capability classes of the soil survey of England and Wales*

CLASS I
Land with very minor or no physical limitations to use

CLASS II
Land with minor limitations that reduce the choice of crops and interfere with cultivations

CLASS III
Land with moderate limitations that restrict the choice of crops and/or demand careful management

CLASS IV
Land with moderately severe limitations that restrict the choice of crop and/or require very careful management practices

CLASS V
Land with severe limitations that restrict its use to pasture, forestry and recreation

CLASS VI
Land with very severe limitations that restrict its use to rough grazing, forestry and recreation

CLASS VII
Land with extremely severe limitations that cannot be rectified

will not affect the classification but major schemes, such as lowering the regional water table, will necessitate a change in classification. Finally it must be appreciated that within classes and subclasses land and the soils may be grouped together for very different reasons and necessitate individual management, fertiliser and cropping programmes.

It has been suggested that this approach stresses the negative features, the limitations, whereas a land capability classification should stress the good properties. A system was proposed several years ago by an American author who used the product of an assessment of four profile characters to give a capability classification, but recently this approach has been expanded by F.A.O. staff to include eight characters. Each factor is rated as a percentage and the product of these gives an index of productivity. When these are adjusted for optimum management, a potentiality index is obtained, thus land is classified on the basis of its 'potentiality' and 'productivity'. Although these approaches can be employed to the greatest advantage in developing countries, their use is still valid in developed countries where land-use decisions are possibly more difficult to make than in a simple economic system.

Soil fertility

When dealing with soils the agricultural aspect always comes to mind first. A soil survey gives an adequate knowledge of the distribution of the soils, their chemical and physical properties. This enables more accurate advice to be given to the farmer regarding fertiliser application to amend plant nutritional deficiencies and lime to correct acidity. At the present time little information is available in Britain about the yield of crops in relation to the specific soils on which they are grown. Figures for overall production can be obtained and farmers are well aware of the productivity of their own land. However, any field or group of fields usually includes several different soils with varied properties and fertility. Some more detailed investigations have been made recently in Britain, but soil scientists in the U.S.A. have been interested in the relationship between crop yield and soils for many years, and yield predictions are a normal outcome of soil survey work.

In an attempt to gain information about the productivity of soils where information is lacking, it is possible to carry out evaluation studies on a few soils which are known to be widespread. These 'benchmark' evaluations can then be extrapolated to similar soils, as it is impracticable to conduct long-term experiments on all soil mapping units, particularly those with a small area of occurrence.

Elements are removed from soils when crops are harvested, pastures grazed or timber removed and at the same time soils lose constituents by the natural process of leaching. Figures for these losses are given as follows:

| Losses | lb/acre annually | | | | | |
	N	P	K	Ca	Mg	S
Leached from a representative silt loam	20	trace	25	100	20	10
Removed by an average rotation crop	120	22	100	40	30	20

Soil fertility has been defined as 'the ability of the soil to supply enough nutrients and water to allow the crop to make the most of the site'. Although the supply of nutrients is a chemical phenomenon, the physical conditions of the soil are also important. In particular, the structure and ability of the soil to supply water, through the medium of which nutrients reach the growing plants. Plant nutrients are present in two forms, available and unavailable. Available nutrients are present in readily assimilable forms which plants can absorb. These are usually present in the soil solution as ions or are adsorbed on the exchange positions of the clay-humus colloids. Two examples of unavailable plant nutrients are of nitrogen which may be locked up in undecomposed plant debris and phosphates which become immobilised as insoluble forms of calcium, iron or aluminium phosphate.

There are about seventeen elements which are essential for satisfactory plant growth. Carbon, hydrogen and oxygen are obtained directly from the atmosphere and the remainder of the macro- and micro-nutrients are derived from the soil. Average amounts of plant nutrients found when surface soils of temperate regions are analysed indicate there to be between 0.20 and 0.50 per cent of nitrogen; 0.01 and 0.20 per cent of phospherus; 0.17 and 3.30 per cent of potassium. The amounts of other element which are utilised by plants include between 0.70 and 3.60 per cent of calcium, 0.12 and 1.50 per cent magnesium and 0.10 and 0.20 per cent of sulphur. Some elements need to be present in the soil in very small amounts or plant growth is unsatisfactory. These 'trace elements' include zinc which ranges between 0.001 and 0.025 per cent, boron and copper 0.0005 and 0.015 per cent and molybdenum 0.00002 and 0.0005 per cent. Although necessary in very small amounts, these heavy metal elements can be toxic to plants if they are present in larger quantities.

Plants need these nutrients in widely differing amounts and a century ago Liebig suggested the ideal fertiliser should contain elements in the same proportion as analysis found them to be present in the plant. Later this was found to be incorrect but the idea of supplying mineral substances to the soil for plant nutrition was conceived. The major nutrients supplied are nitrogen,

phosphorus and potassium and many granulated artificial fertilisers are available commercially from which farmers and horticulturalists can select one suitable for increasing the level of fertility of their soil depending on the crop to be grown.

For many years the supply of nitrogen to plant was not understood. Liebig's theory of supplying the plant with its nutrients had discounted the limited availability of nitrogen and his patent manure did not contain nitrogen compounds. It was not until the end of the nineteenth century that scientists in Germany showed that nitrogen was 'fixed' by micro-organisms living free in the soil or symbiotically in root nodules of leguminous plants.

Nitrogen is closely linked to the amount of vegetative growth, so additions of nitrogenous fertiliser increase the bulk of forage crops but can delay ripening in cereals and leave the crop susceptible to fungal attack. Shortage of nitrogen can be seen by a yellow colour of the foliage combined with lack of growth. In natural conditions nitrogen is obtained primarily from the

12.2 The nitrogen cycle

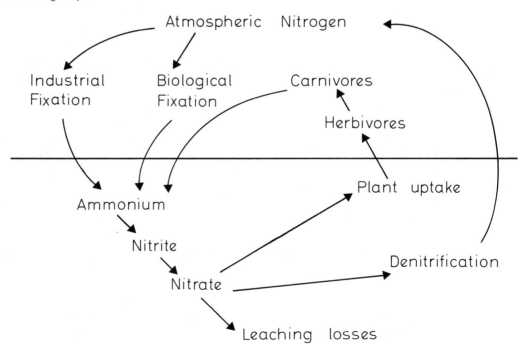

atmosphere through the action of symbiotic bacteria living in association with the roots of leguminous plants such as beans, peas, vetches and clovers. Other plants, for example sea buckthorn and cycads, also have a similar symbiotic relationship and there are free-living nitrogen fixing bacteria in the soil. Before the invention of artificial fertilisers nitrogen was obtained for crops mainly by the decomposition of animal and vegetable material by bacterial attack in the soil releasing ammonia which further breaks down to nitrates in the well-known nitrogen cycle Fig. 12.2).

Phosphorus also occurs naturally as an element in breakdown products of plant or animal matter and in this form is most readily available for crops. Inorganic calcium phosphate, such as the mineral apatite, occurs in many localities throughout the world. When finely ground and spread on the soil it is referred to as 'rock phosphate' which slowly releases phosphate when it weathers. Bones were used by J. B. Lawes when he ran out of local naturally occurring phosphate deposits in his early attempts to make 'superphosphate' fertiliser with sulphuric acid on his estate. Subsequently he used imported calcium phosphate. The revenue from his patent later was used to endow Rothamsted Experimental Station at Harpenden in England. Commercial production of triple superphosphate fertiliser now takes place by the action of orthophosphoric acid on rock phosphate yielding about 50 per cent soluble P_2O_5. Unfortunately, when it is added to the soil, much of the phosphate is immobilised as insoluble phosphates of iron, calcium and aluminium and is unavailable for the growing plants. An alternative source of phosphate, also industrial, is a by-product of the process of making steel from pig-iron. Phosphate impurities are combined with calcium as 'basic slag', which when poured off, cooled and ground can be used directly as a fertiliser. It is particularly favoured for use on permanent or ley pastures in leaching environments where the addition of calcium helps to maintain a satisfactory pH range. Root crops, particularly swedes, turnips and potatoes are sensitive to a lack of phosphorus. More rapid growth in the early stages and better tillering is obtained in cereal crops by the application of this plant nutrient. It is involved in the formation of cell nucleoproteins as well as in the metabolism of carbohydrates.

The third major plant nutrient is potassium. In rocks, potassium occurs in silicate minerals such as orthoclase and mica as well as in evaporites deposited as inland seas dried. The common name, potash, derives from the concentrated leachate of wood ash, chiefly potassium carbonate, from which this element was formerly derived. Although potassium salts readily dissolve in water, not all the potassium applied in fertiliser is immediately available as some becomes adsorbed on the clay-humus complex. The process of base exchange then allows a steady release over a period of time which can be taken up by the growing plants or is lost in the drainage waters. Potassium is utilised by plants in their metabolic processes, particularly in the building of amino acids and proteins. When deficiency occurs leaf tips and margins can be seen to be dying prematurely and plants are small with low yields.

Although it is vital to have the correct balance of available plant nutrients, it is essential that the soil is neither too acid nor too alkaline because the availability of nutrients and trace elements is limited at extremes of pH value. It is also important for the soil to have a good physical condition, as without stable soil structure, drainage is impaired and the diffusion of oxygen into, and carbon dioxide out of, the soil is restricted. Modern intensive forms of agriculture, with monocultures of crops such as barley, have tended to reduce the amount of organic matter and so weaken soil structure. At the same time agricultural machinery has become heavier, compressing and compacting the soil. Clearly, this is a problem which must be kept under surveillance or optimum yields will not be obtained, even where nutrients are present in the correct proportions.

Arid and semi-arid countries have limited food production because of a lack of water and facilities for irrigation. At present approximately 126 million hectares are irrigated, 75 per cent of which is in Asia and 12 per cent in North and Central America. This represents approximately 9 per cent of the total amount of arable land in the world, and it is further estimated that there are 255 million hectares, situated mainly in the

12.3 Salt efflorescence, southern Tunisia

U.S.S.R. and Asia, which might be used in future developments.

Although in many cases water can be made available, before an irrigation scheme is built and put into practice it is necessary first of all to assess the soils of the area for their suitability for irrigation and the soluble salt content of the water supply. The topographic situation of the scheme must be considered, for water must be brought easily to the site. The under-drainage must be satisfactory or ground-water levels will rise and salinity will occur in the soils (Fig. 12.3).

12.4 A top-dressing trial with sugar beet

All farming systems attempt to utilise the soil for crop production on a continuing basis. A simple system, such as shifting cultivation or bush fallow allows a natural regeneration of fertility under wild vegetation. Burning them releases the combined plant nutrients which fertilise the succeeding crop. Unfortunately there are always losses of nutrients and fertility rapidly declines, particularly in tropical soils. The three field system of medieval farmers in western Europe delayed the exhaustion of their cultivated land by rotation of crops and a fallow period. The agricultural crop rotations developed in the eighteenth century including the famous 'Norfolk Fourcourse' combined the effect of fallowing with a root crop and, by the use of clovers and grasses which were grazed, ensured at least some residual fertility for the succeeding grain crop. The use of artificial fertilisers has assisted agriculturalists greatly, increasing yields and also replacing elements removed from the soil by crops as well as reducing the dependence on farm yard manure. Rotation of crops is still beneficial because without it disease and pests increase. Ley grasses and the addition of organic matter to the soil also assist maintenance of a good soil structure, essential for the promotion of good aeration and drainage in the soil. Over-use of fertilisers can be harmful as it leads to eutrophication of rivers and lakes, a process whereby rapid plant growth can lead to deoxygenation and the death of all life in those bodies of water. Drinking water supplies can be affected by nitrates which are harmful particularly to very young children. For both health and economy, fertilisers should not be applied at levels in excess of those found by experimentation to be justified by economic returns (Fig. 12.4).

Other applications of soil science

In those countries with large areas still undeveloped or at a low level of production, the apportionment or reapportionment of the land could be an important sequel to natural resource surveys, including soil surveys. Perhaps the best known series of surveys of this type are those done by the Land Research Division of C.S.I.R.O. in Australasia. The landscape is analysed into 'land systems' each of which has an individual pattern of geology, topography, soils and vegetaion, p. 105. In this way an undeveloped area can be assessed, together with its climate, for its potentialities. In particular its broad use for agriculture, grazing, forestry and communications can be forecast. Subsequently detailed surveys can identify specific development projects such as an irrigation scheme, pasture improvement or forestry development. Similar surveys are carried out by the Directorate of Overseas Surveys in Commonwealth Countries. In the Netherlands, surveys have been made of the newly drained polders of the Ijsselmeer, where land-use plans based on soil surveys have been drawn up for the lands originally beneath the sea.

The soil scientist can assist in the reclamation of eroded and derelict land. Large areas of the world are affected by salinity or have suffered soil erosion through over-exploitation, as in America, Russia and Brazil. The maintenance of the physical characteristics of the soil are as important as its fertility, as with a breakdown of structure soils are liable to be eroded away easily. Soil scientists co-operate with farmers and agricultural advisors to work out the best cropping and cultivation programme commensurate with soil conservation. Terracing, strip-cropping, shelterbelts, special types and times of cultivation and maintenance of reasonable levels of organic matter are all encouraged by soil scientists in an attempt to counteract soil erosion by wind and water. Areas which have been mined by the opencast method for coal, lignite, ironstone, gravel and many other minerals, can be restored to a productive capacity. Soil scientists, in collaboration with agriculturalists, foresters and ecologists can help to accelerate the natural processes of revegetation and return to usefulness (Fig. 12.5).

Increasing knowledge of the soil may in future take a larger part in the valuation of land for agricultural and horticultural purposes. Obviously the soil already plays an important part in a prospective buyer's assessment of a market price, although his assessment is usually based upon instinct rather than upon an accurate knowledge of the soils on a property. Perhaps in future years the Inland Revenue may use the land capability category as a basis on which to assess tax liability.

12.5(a) An opencast coal site (b) A restored site with new fences, ditches and pasture

As the natural timber resources of the world are being consumed many countries have to consider replanting their forests on a fairly large scale. Whilst many foresters know by experience where certain species of tree will grow satisfactorily, newly acquired areas can be planted with a much greater confidence of success if conditions of the soil site and semi-natural vegetation are known in advance. Recent work by the British Forestry Commission Site Survey Section has generated a soil-site classification which aims to establish a grouping of soils for silvicultural use in their forests. It is anticipated that these site types, which are based on soil characteristics, drainage, exposure, cultivation need and fertiliser requirement, drought and pollution liability, will allow predictions to be made of future management and crop performance. Similar soil-site survey techniques have been developed in the United States and Canada where they are widely used for all types of afforestation.

In times of strategic necessity, information can be provided by soil maps about the feasibility of the terrain for military vehicles, or for the location of roads or airfields. In times of peace, the same interpretation can be used for civil engineering undertakings. This has given rise to the development of a new branch of applied landscape studies called terrain evaluation. This has three aspects: analysis, involving the understanding of the natural environment; classification, characterising and distinguishing areas from each other and appraisal, the interpretation and assessment of data for practical purposes.

Town and country planners can use information on the soil at all levels of their work. At the level of regional planning, the overall policy will require information to enable land to be allocated for residential, commercial, industrial, agricultural and recreational development. At a local level the siting of houses, schools, and other buildings may well be determined by the soil distribution, particularly if cracking, heaving clay soils occur. In rural areas, away from a mains sewerage scheme, disposal of sewage in septic tanks can provide problems if the soils and sub-soils are not sufficiently permeable. In the past, planning of suburban areas has taken too little cognisance of the natural environment

in the development of new housing areas. The American soil scientist Kellogg has written 'People have no need whatever to put their houses where they will slide down hill, settle and crack or be flooded; nor where their gardens will be contaminated with sewage effluent; nor where their homes cannot be beautified with growing plants. It has been demonstrated that what has been learned about soil selection for the many specialities in farming can be used for these other purposes'.

Given adequate information about soils and landscape, soundly based proposals can be advanced for the most satisfactory re-development and utilisation of the land. Examples in Yorkshire, England, include the use of poorly drained soils on river terraces as wildlife and nature reserves with footpaths on the better drained areas and possibly further excavation of poorly drained land to provide filling or a covering medium in the restoration of colliery waste. Other thin superficial deposits overlying Coal Measures shales could be best developed for housing or light industrial use as heavy industrial building would mean greatly increased costs in foundation work if differential subsidence were to be avoided. The case for retaining existing woodland in preference to other uses could be argued from the soil and other physical attributes of the site as removal of the trees would make natural drainage conditions even worse than those which exist at present.

A greater knowledge of the soils of the world brings with it a better insight into ecological relationships. The dependence of agriculture and forestry on the soil has already been mentioned, but equally important are the nature reserves and water catchment areas which are of great amenity value. The soil scientist can contribute a valuable opinion on the management and use of such areas. Frequently, these areas serve a dual purpose. With increasing leisure time, the management of recreational land becomes more important. Soil surveys can give information as to the best areas for camp sites, games areas and trails throughout nature reserves.

Pedology is a correlative science, bringing together the many facets of the environment as they are involved in the formation and main enance of the soil. It is a young science and has within it room for many different scientific approaches. The information of soil science can be used by many people in agriculture, archaeology, civil engineering, plant and animal ecology, and forestry. It should play a greater part in geographical appraisal and planning decisions of local and national authorities.

BOOKS AND JOURNALS FOR FURTHER READING

This book attempts to include the basic material for an introductory course in pedology and soil geography. There are numerous textbooks on the subject of soil science or pedology, some of which are mentioned in the following section but, although each has its specific merits, these books are frequently written from an agronomic point of view. Articles concerning soil development and soil distribution occur scattered throughout scientific journals published in many different countries of the world, and those readily available to an English-speaking student are as follows. In Britain, the British Society of Soil Science publishes the *Journal of Soil Science* and a recent addition has been *Earth Surface Processes*. The abstract journal, *Soils and Fertilizers* contains classified abstracts from the literature of soil science and frequently has a useful review or leading article. Three major English language journals are published in North America. *Soil Science* and the *Proceedings of the Soil Science Society of America* are printed in the United States, and Canadian soil scientists contribute to the *Canadian Journal of Soil Science*. Articles printed in English frequently appear in European journals: *Geoderma* is published in the Netherlands, *Catena* in West Germany and *Pedologie* in Belgium. The Russian journal is *Pochvovedenie*, translated as *Soviet Soil Science* in the United States.

The national soil survey organisations of most countries produce memoirs or bulletins to accompany their soil maps and the World Soil Resources Office of the Food and Agricultural Organisation also publishes information about soils and their distribution. As a fundamental basis for crop production, forestry, and many geographical distributions, articles about soils can be found scattered throughout their journals. The following list of books and journals has been found useful by the author and is based upon an article entitled 'Soil Geography, its Content and Literature' published in the *Journal of Geography in Higher Education*, 1, 61–72. The choice is personal, and by no means comprehensive, but the articles listed can be used both for further reading or as starting points for tutorial discussions in more advanced courses.

Chapter 1
Cline, M. J. 1961. The changing model of soils. *Proc. Soil. Sci. Amer.* 25, 442–6.

Eyre, S. R. 1968. *Vegetation and Soils*. Edward Arnold, London.

Russell, E. J. 1957. *The World of the Soil*. New Naturalist Series, Collins, London.

Simonson, R. W. 1959. Outline of a generalised theory of soil genesis. *Proc. Soil Sci. Soc. Amer.* 23, 152–6.

Stewart, A. B. 1965. Soil in the field and in the laboratory. *J. Soil Sci.* 16, 171–82.

Williamson, W. T. H. 1959. The discipline of soil science. *J. Soil Sci.* 10, 1–4.

Chapter 2
Brady, N. C. 1974. *The Nature and Properties of Soils*. Macmillan, London.

Duchaufour, P. 1971. *Précis de Pédologie* (2nd Edition). Masson et Cie, Paris.

Foth, H. D. & Turk, L. M. 1972. *Fundamentals of Soil Science*. (5th Edition). John Wiley, New York.

Gerasimov, I. P. & Glazovskaya, M. A. 1965. *Fundamentals of Soil Science and Soil Geography*. Tr. A. Gourevitch. Israel Programme for Scientific Translations, Jerusalem.

Joffe, J. 1949. *Pedology*. Pedology Publications, New Brunswick; New Jersey, U.S.A.

Russell, E. W. 1973. *Soil Conditions and Plant Growth*. (10th Edition). Longmans, London.

Townsend, W. N. 1973. *An Introduction to the Scientific Study of the Soil*. (5th Edition). Edward Arnold, London.

Chapter 3
Bidwell, O. & Hole, F. D. 1965. Man as a factor of soil formation. *Soil Sci.* 99, 65–72.

Bridges E. M. 1978. Interaction of soil and mankind in Britain *J. Soil Sci.* 29, 125–39.

Jenny, H. 1941. *Factors of Soil Formation*. McGraw-Hill, New York.

Landsberg, H. E. and Blanc, M. L. 1958. Interaction of soil and weather. *Proc. Soil Sci. Soc. Amer.* 22, 491–5.

Chapter 4
Buol, S. W., Hole, F. D. & McCracken, R. J. 1973. *Soil Genesis and Classification*. Iowa State University Press, Ames, Iowa.

Chapter 5

Aubert, G. 1965. La classification pedologique utilisée en France. *Pedologie*, No. Spec. 3, 25–51.

Avery, B. W. 1973. Soil classification in the Soil Survey of England and Wales. *J. Soil Sci.* 24, 324–38.

Bidwell, O. & Hole, F. D. 1964. Numerical taxonomy and soil classification. *Soil Sci.* 97, 58–62.

Buol, S. W., Hole, F. D. & McCracken, R. J. 1973. *Soil Genesis and Classification*. Iowa State University Press, Ames, Iowa.

Cuanalo, H. E. de la, & Webster, R. 1970. A comparative study of numerical classification and ordination of soil profiles in a locality near Oxford. *J. Soil Sci.* 21, 339–52.

F.A.O./U.N.E.S.C.O. 1974. *Soil Map of the World, 1:5,000,000*. Vol. 1 Legend. U.N.E.S.C.O. Paris.

Ganssen, R. & Hadrich, F. 1965. *Atlas zur Bodenkunde*. Bibliographisches Institut. Mannheim. (German text, but maps have key in English, French, Spanish and Russian.)

Hallsworth, E. G. 1965. *Experimental Pedology*. Ed. Hallsworth and Crawford, D. V. Butterworths, London.

Kaurichev, I. S. & Gromiko, I. D. 1974. *Atlas Pochv S.S.S.R.* Kolos, Moscow.

Kubiena, W. L. 1953. *The Soils of Europe*. Murby, London.

Northcote, K. 1965. *A Factual Key for the Recognition of Australian Soils*. C.S.I.R.O. Divisional Report 1960. 2nd Edition. Adelaide.

Ragg, J. M. & Clayden, B. 1973. The classification of some British soils according to the comprehensive system of the United States. *Tech. Monogr.* 3. Soil Survey of England and Wales, Harpenden.

Robinson, G. W. 1949. *Soils, their origin, constitution and classification*. Murby, London.

Simonson, R. W. 1962. Soil classification in the United States. *Science*, 137, 1027–34.

Soil Survey Staff, 1975. *Soil Taxonomy*. Agriculture Handbook 436 U.S.D.A., Washington.

Tiurin, I. V. 1965. The system of soil classification in the U.S.S.R. *Pedologie*, No. Spec. 3, 7–20.

Chapter 6

Dimbleby, G. W. 1952. Pleistocene ice wedges in N.E. Yorkshire. *J. Soil Sci.* 3, 1–19.

Fitzpatrick, E. A. 1956. An indurated horizon formed by permafrost. *J. Soil Sci.* 7, 248–54.

Hill, D. E. & Tedrow, J. C. F. 1961. Weathering and soil formation in the arctic environment. *Amer. J. Sci.*, 259, 84–101.

Smith, J. 1956. Some moving soils in Spitzbergen. *J. Soil Sci.* 7, 10–21.

Svatkov, N. M. 1958. Soils of Wrangel Island. *Sov. Soil Sci.* (Jan), 80–7.

Tedrow, J. C. F. *et al.* 1958. Major genetic soils of the Arctic slope of Alaska. *J. Soil Sci.* 9, 33–45.

Chapter 7

The System of Soil Classification for Canada. 1970 Canada Dept. Agriculture, Ottawa.

Avery, B. W. 1958. A sequence of beechwood soils on the Chiltern Hills, England. *J. Soil Sci.* 9, 210–24.

Ball, D. F. 1966. Brown podzolic soils and their status in Britain. *J. Soil Sci.* 17, 148–58.

Curtis, L. F., Courtney, F. M. & Trudgill, S. T. 1976. *Soils in the British Isles*. Longman, London.

Mackney, D. 1961. A podzol development sequence in oakwoods and heath in central England. *J. Soil Sci.* 12, 23–40.

Muir, A. 1961. The podzol and podzolic soils. *Advances in Agronomy*, 13, 1–56.

Muir, J. W. 1955. The effect of soil-forming factors over an area in the south of Scotland. *J. Soil Sci.* 6, 84–93.

Stobbe, P. C. & Wright, J. R. 1959. Modern concepts of the genesis of podzols. *Proc. Soil Sci. Soc. Amer.* 23, 161–4.

See also *Memoirs of Soil Survey of England and Wales*. Harpenden. *Memoirs of Soil Survey of Scotland*. Macaulay Institute, Aberdeen.

Chapter 8

Afanasyeva, E. A. 1966. Thick chernozem under grass and tree cenoses. *Sov. Soil Sci.* (June), 615–25.

Aubert, G. 1962. Arid zone soils. A study of their formation, characteristics, utilization and conservation. *Arid Zone Res.* 18, 115–37.

Aubert, G. & Boulaine, J. 1967. *La Pédologie*. Que Sais-je? Presses Universitaires de France, Paris.

Buol, S. W. 1965. Present soil forming factors and processes in arid and semi-arid regions. *Soil Sci.* 99, 45–9.

McClelland, J. E. *et al.* 1959. Chernozems of eastern North Dakota. *Proc. Soil Sci. Soc. Amer.* 23, 51–6

McCaleb, S. G. 1959. The genesis of red-yellow podzolic soils. *Proc. Soil Sci. Soc. Amer.* 23, 164–8.

Northcote, K. H. *et al.* 1975. *A Description of Australian Soils*. C.S.I.R.O, Adelaide, South Australia.

Stace H. C. T. *et al.* 1968. *A Handbook of Australian Soils*, Rellim Technical Publications, Glenside, South Australia.

Chapter 9

Buringh, P. 1970. *Introduction to the Study of Soils in Tropical and Subtropical Regions*. Pudoc, Wageningen, Netherlands.

Cunningham, R. K. 1963. The effect of clearing a tropical forest soil. *J. Soil Sci.* 14, 334–5.

Ellis, B. S. 1952. Genesis of a tropical red soil. *J. Soil Sci.* 3, 52–62.

D'Hoore, J. L. 1964. *Soil map of Africa, 1:5,000,000*. C.T.C.A., Lagos.

Kalpage, F.S.C.P. 1976. *Tropical Soils*. Macmillan, London.

Klinge, H. 1965. Podzol soils in the Amazon Basin. *J. Soil Sci.* 16, 95–103.

McNeil, M. 1964. Lateritic soils. *Scientific American*, 207 (11), 97–102.

Mohr, E. C. J., Baren, F. A. van & Schuylenborch, J. van, 1972. *Tropical Soils.* Mouten-Ichtiar Bara-Van Hoere, The Hague.

Mulcahy, M. J. 1960. Laterites and lateritic soils in South-western Australia. *J. Soil Sci.* 11, 206–25.

Nye, P. H. 1954. Some soil forming processes in the humid tropics. 1. A field study of a catena in the West African Forest. *J. Soil Sci.* 5, 7–21.

Watson, J. P. 1964. A soil catena on granite in Southern Rhodesia. 1. Field observations. *J. Soil Sci.* 15, 238–50.

Whitmore, T. C. 1975. *Tropical Rainforests of the Far East*, Clarendon Press, Oxford.

Young, A. 1976. *Tropical Soils and Soil Survey.* Cambridge University Press.

Chapter 10

Avery, B. W. 1958. A sequence of beechwood soils on the Chiltern Hills, England. *J. Soil Sci.* 9, 210–24.

Crompton, E. 1952. Some morphological features associated with poor soil drainage. *J. Soil. Sci.* 3, 277–89.

Chapter 11

Beckett, P. H. T. & Clarke, G. R. 1972. *The Study of the Soil in the Field.* (5th Edition) Oxford University Press, Oxford.

Hodgson, J. M. 1978. *Soil Sampling and soil description.* Oxford University Press.

Milne, G. 1936. *A Soil Reconnaissance through parts of Tanganyika Territory.* Memoirs Agric. Res. Sta., Amani. Reprinted in *J. Ecol.* 35, 192.

Perry, R. A. *et al.* 1962. *General Report on Lands of the Alice Spring Area, Northern Territory, 1956–57.* (Land Research Series 6.) C.S.I.R.O., Melbourne.

Soil Survey Staff. 1974. *Soil Survey Field Handbook.* Soil Survey of England and Wales. Harpenden, England.

See also *Memoirs of Soil Survey of England and Wales.* Harpenden. *Memoirs of Soil Survey of Scotland.* Macaulay Institute, Aberdeen.

Chapter 12

Baren, F. A. van 1960. Soils in relation to population in tropical regions. *Tijd. voor econ. en Soc. Geog.* 51, 230–3.

Bartelli, L. J. *et al.* 1966. *Soil Surveys and Land Use Planning.* Soil Sci. Sco. Amer., Madison.

Beek, K. J. 1978. *Land Evaluation for Agricultural Development.* Pub. 23 International Institute for Land Reclamation and Improvement.

Bibby, J. S. & Mackney, D. 1969. *Land Use Capability Classification. Tech. Monogr.* 1. Soil Survey of England and Wales, Harpenden.

F.A.O. 1976. *A Framework for Land Evaluation.* Pub. 22 International Institute for Land Reclamation and Improvement.

Jacks, G, V. 1956. *Soil.* Nelson & Sons Ltd, London.

Klingebiel, A. A. & Montgomery, P. H. 1962. *Land Capability Classfication.* U.S. Dept. Agric. Handbook No. 210, Washington.

Simonson, R. W. (Ed.) 1974. Non-agricultural applications of soil surveys. Developments in soil science 4. (Reprint from *Geoderma* 10). Elsevier. Amsterdam.

Yaalon, D. H. & Yaron, B. 1966. Framework for manmade soil changes – an outline of metapedogenesis. *Soil Sci.* 102, 272–7.

INDEX

calcium carbonate, 25, 61, 70, 78, 91
  concretions, 70, 71, 75
cambic horizon, 31, 40–1, 60, 63–4
Cambisol, 44, 53, 58, 91
  Calcic, 52
  Dystric, 53, 60, 61, 62
  Eutric, 53, 60, 61
  Gelic, 49
  Gleyic, 94, 97
capillary movement of water, 22
carbon dioxide, 20, 96
catena, 26, 49, 81, 101, 103
chernozem, 19, 25, 44, 64, 65, 73–6, 91, 99, 101, 102, 110
calcic chernozem, 75
chestnut soil, 25, 76–7, 99, 102, 109
cinnamon soil, 67, 70
classification of soils, by
  Avery, 44–5
  Commission de Pedologie (France), 39
  F.A.O./U.N.E.S.C.O., 43–4
  Hallsworth, 43
  Northcote, 40
  Robinson, 38
  U.S. Soil Taxonomy, 41
clay, 14–16
clay humus complex, 19, 31, 34, 95, 113, 115
clay minerals, 17, 18, 27, 43, 81
  hydrous micas, 17
  kaolinite, 17, 34, 71, 82, 83
  montmorillonite, 17, 18, 27, 36, 87
climate and soil formation, 9, 10, 24, 28, 47, 48, 54, 61, 64, 71, 72, 73, 74, 77–8, 80–1
  brown earth, 61
  chermozem, 74
  desert soil, 77–8
  grey soil, 64
  Mediterranean soil, 67–8
  podzol, 54
  red-yellow podzolic soil, 71
  tropical soil, 80–1
  tundra soil, 47–8
climatic change, 28, 66, 73
Colembollae (spring tails), 19, 25, 26
colloids, 18, 19, 32, 113
concreations, 18, 70, 71, 75, 89, 94
conservation, 117
convolutions, 51
croûte calcaire, 71
cryoturbation, 49

D

definition of soil, 10
derno podzolic soil, 60, 62

desert lac, 78
desert pavement, 79
desert soil, 77–9, 99, 101, 109
Dokuchaiev, 10, 11, 24, 37, 107
duricrust, 81 (silcrete)
duripan, 40

E

earthworms, 18, 19, 61
eluvial horizon, 11, 12, 31, 32, 33, 40, 50, 55, 56, 57, 58, 60, 63, 65
eluviation, 30, 31
Entisol, 41, 51, 67, 79, 98
  Aquent, 41, 88, 93
  Arent, 41
  Fluvaquent 98
  Fluvent, 41, 53
  Orthent, 41, 53
  Psamment, 41
  Quartzipsamment 86, 98
epipedon, 40
  anthropic, 40
  histic, 40
  mollic, 40, 41, 73
  ochric, 40, 41
  plaggen, 40
  umbric, 40
erg, 79
erosion, 68, 81, 89, 92, 117
erosion surfaces, 80
Eurasia, 47, 54, 77, 109
Europe, 25, 43, 51, 55, 56, 58, 60, 61, 65, 68, 92, 106, 110
  Ardennes, 62
  Balkans, 70
  Britain, 18, 26, 28, 43, 51, 56, 58, 61, 63, 92, 100, 105, 106, 107, 112, 113
  Cyprus, 71
  England, 27, 36, 52, 56, 60, 63, 92, 94, 115
  Finistère, 62
  France, 39, 62, 63, 100
  Georgia, 22, 72
  Germany, 92, 114
  Holland, 55, 97, 99, 117
  Hungary, 73
  Mediterranean basin, 67, 68
  Norway, 47
  Paris basin, 60, 62
  Romania, 73
  Russia, 18, 32, 51, 54, 56, 58, 64, 65, 73, 75, 77, 78, 116, 117
  Scotland, 27, 28, 51, 103
  Spain, 70
  Spitzbergen, 48, 49
  Ukraine, 73, 76, 97
  Wales, 27, 28, 51, 52
evapotranspiration, 26

exchangeable ions, 19, 22, 30, 34, 96–7
exchange capacity, 19

F

factors of soil formation, 24
  climate, 24–5
  organisms, 25–6
  relief, 26
  parent material, 26–7
  time, 27–8
faecal pellets, 19
fen peat, 27, 36, 100
ferrallitic soil, 27, 82, 83, 99, 109, 110
ferrallitization, 30, 33, 34, 71, 73
Ferralsol, 44, 82, 86, 99
  Acric, 83
  Humic, 99
  Orthic, 83
  Xanthic, 99
ferric oxide, 17, 81, 85, 93, 95
Ferrod, 42, 53
ferruginous tropical soil, 27, 82, 83, 109, 110
fertilizers, 26, 110, 111, 113, 114, 115, 116
festoons (convolutions or involutions), 51
field capacity, 22
fine earth, 14
Fluvent, 41, 53
Fluvisol, 43, 53, 88, 91, 98
  Thionic, 87
fragipan, 40
fragmental, 17
free survey, 105–6
fungi, 54

G

garrigue, 68
gilgai, 87
gleying, 22, 27, 30, 34, 35, 38, 56, 58, 93–5
  ground water gley, 35, 93–5
  surface water gley, 35, 63, 93–4
Gleysol, 43, 93
  Dystric, 58
  Gelic, 50, 51
grey brown podzolic soil, 53, 60
grey forest soil, 65
grey desert soil (sierozem), 25, 78, 99
grey soil, 53, 64, 65
grey wooded soil, 64
Greyzem, 44
  Orthic, 53, 65
gypsic horizon, 40

H

Hallsworth, 43
halomorphic soil, 91, 95–7, 99

podzols, 54
red-yellow podzolic soils, 71
tropical soils, 81
tundra soils, 48
Vertisol, 27, 44, 82–3, 86–7
   Torrert, 41
   Udert, 41
   Ustert, 41, 71
   Xerert, 41, 71

W

warping, 99
weathering, 27, 29, 30, 48, 78, 80,
   81, 83

weathered mantle, 13
   weathering factor, 25
white alkali soil, 34, 51, 95, 96
World Soil Map, 102

X

Xeralf, 42
Xerert, 41, 71
Xeroll, 42, 73
Xerosol, 44, 78
   Calcic, 78, 95
   Gypsic, 78, 95
   Haplic, 78
   Luvic, 78

Xerult, 42, 73

Y

yellow earth, 82
yellow latosol, 85
Yermosol, 44, 78, 91
   Calcic, 79
   Gypsic, 95
young soil, 37, 79

Z

zheltozem, 82
zonal classification, 37, 46
zones, geographical, 10, 45–6